GOODSON MUMBA

DEVELOPMENTAL STUDIES

An Interdisciplinary Approach in the Zambian Context

Contents

Preface — iv
Acknowledgement — vii
Dedication — viii
Disclaimer — ix

1 Chapter 1: Introduction to Developmental Studies in Zambia — 1
2 Chapter 2: Theories of Development — 14
3 Chapter 3: Economic Development — 31
4 Chapter 4: Social Development — 45
5 Chapter 5: Political Development — 58
6 Chapter 6: Environmental Sustainability — 74
7 Chapter 7: Cultural Dimensions of Development — 91
8 Chapter 8: Global Health and Development — 108
9 Chapter 9: Education and Development — 126
10 Chapter 10: Gender and Development — 144
11 Chapter 11: Rural Development — 163
12 Chapter 12: Urban Development — 183
13 Chapter 13: Technology and Development — 203
14 Chapter 14: Development Policy and Planning — 223
15 Chapter 15: Case Studies in Development — 244
About the Author — 264

Preface

In the dynamic landscape of Zambia, where the interplay of historical legacies, cultural richness, economic potential, and social challenges presents a unique developmental tapestry, there arises a pressing need for a comprehensive and nuanced understanding of the country's developmental journey. This book, "Developmental Studies: An Interdisciplinary Approach in the Zambian Context," seeks to address this need by offering a holistic exploration of Zambia's developmental trajectory through an interdisciplinary lens.

The genesis of this book stems from a profound recognition of the interconnectedness of various dimensions of development—economic, social, political, environmental, and cultural. In Zambia, these dimensions are intricately woven together, influencing and shaping each other in ways that are both complex and compelling. To unravel this complexity, it is imperative to adopt an interdisciplinary approach that transcends the boundaries of traditional academic disciplines, allowing for a more integrated and comprehensive analysis.

Our journey through the pages of this book begins with an exploration of the foundational concepts and historical context of development in Zambia. From there, we delve into the major theories of development, examining their applicability and relevance to the Zambian context. The subsequent chapters provide an in-depth analysis of key areas such as economic growth, social development, political governance, environmental sustainability, and cultural dimensions, each interwoven with real-life stories and case studies that bring the theoretical concepts to life.

Throughout this book, we have endeavored to highlight the importance of local context and indigenous knowledge in shaping development pathways. The voices and perspectives of Zambian communities, policymakers, scholars, and practitioners are central to this narrative, providing valuable insights and practical examples of development challenges and successes. By doing so, we aim to foster a deeper understanding of the diverse and dynamic nature of development in Zambia.

As we stand at the crossroads of unprecedented global challenges and opportunities, the role of interdisciplinary approaches in addressing complex developmental issues has never been more critical. This book aspires to contribute to the ongoing discourse on development in Zambia by offering a comprehensive, contextually relevant, and forward-looking perspective. It is our hope that this work will serve as a valuable resource for students, researchers, policymakers, development practitioners, and anyone with a keen interest in the multifaceted journey of Zambia's development.

In conclusion, we extend our heartfelt gratitude to all those who have contributed to the creation of this book. To the scholars whose research forms the foundation of our analysis, to the communities whose stories bring depth and richness to our narrative, and to the readers who engage with these pages with an open mind and a spirit of inquiry—we thank you. Together, let us embark on this journey of discovery, reflection, and action towards a more inclusive, equitable, and

sustainable future for Zambia.
Best Regards,
Goodson Mumba

Acknowledgement

I would like to eternally and gratefully acknowledge the Almighty God for the infinite intelligence from His universal mind where we draw from all that we come to know and are yet to know. May I also acknowledge and thank everyone that has played a part in my journey of life in terms of spiritual, moral, emotional and material support.

Dedication

I extend my sincerest gratitude to my beloved wife, Edith Mumba, and our children, Angelina, Lubuto, Letticia, Lulumbi, and Butusho, for their unwavering support and understanding throughout the conception, writing, and eventual publication of this book, despite the sacrifices and challenges they endured.

Disclaimer

1

Chapter 1: Introduction to Developmental Studies in Zambia

Definition and Scope in the Zambian Context

I n the bustling halls of the University of Zambia, Dr. Mwansa, an esteemed professor of Developmental Studies, stood before a class of eager students, the air buzzing with anticipation.

"Welcome, class, to the heart of our journey," Dr. Mwansa began, his voice commanding attention. "Today, we embark on a quest to unravel the essence of developmental studies within the rich tapestry of Zambia."

As he paced the room, his eyes sparkled with enthusiasm. "Development," he proclaimed, "is not merely the growth of infrastructure or the rise of GDP. It is the intricate dance of progress, equity, and sustainability."

With a flourish, he unveiled a map of Zambia, its contours illuminated under the classroom lights. "Here lies our canvas," he declared, sweeping his hand across the map. "From the copper-laden soils of the Copperbelt to the tranquil banks of the Zambezi River, Zambia's terrain is our laboratory, our muse."

Gesturing towards the eager faces before him, he continued, "But what, my dear students, defines the scope of our inquiry? What is development in the Zambian context?"

A hush fell over the room as Dr. Mwansa's words hung in the air, heavy with anticipation. "Development," he began, his voice resonating with conviction, "is the pursuit of a better tomorrow for all Zambians, irrespective of creed or circumstance. It is the promise of prosperity, dignity, and empowerment."

With each word, he painted a vivid portrait of hope and possibility. "Development knows no bounds from the bustling streets of Lusaka to the verdant plains of Eastern Province. It encompasses economic growth, social equity, political stability, and environmental stewardship."

The students nodded in understanding, their minds ablaze with newfound clarity. "But remember," Dr. Mwansa cautioned, his tone imbued with gravitas, "development is not a destination, but a journey. And as scholars of developmental studies, it is our solemn duty to navigate this path with humility, empathy, and unwavering resolve."

With a final glance at the map before him, Dr. Mwansa concluded, "So let us embark on this odyssey together, as guardians of Zambia's future, seekers of truth, and champions of progress."

And with that, the journey began—a journey fuelled by curiosity, guided by wisdom, and bound by the unbreakable spirit of Zambia's quest for development.

Historical Context and Evolution of Development in Zambia

As the sun dipped below the horizon, casting an amber glow over the campus, Dr. Mwansa's voice echoed through the corridors of the lecture hall, captivating his students with tales of Zambia's storied past.

"With each step forward," he began, his voice steeped in reverence, "we must first look back—to the crucible of history that forged the Zambia we know today."

The students leaned in, their hearts quickening with anticipation, as Dr. Mwansa conjured images of a bygone era—a time when Zambia was known as Northern Rhodesia, shackled by the chains of colonialism.

"Once, our land echoed with the cries of oppression," he intoned, his words heavy with the weight of centuries. "But from the ashes of subjugation rose the flames of independence—a beacon of hope, illuminating the path to self-determination."

With a flick of his hand, Dr. Mwansa summoned images of jubilant crowds, waving flags of green, red, and black—a symphony of liberation reverberating across the land. "In 1964, Zambia emerged from the crucible of colonial rule, a phoenix reborn—a nation united in its quest for freedom, justice, and prosperity."

The students nodded in solemn recognition, their minds transported to a time of upheaval and transformation. "But our journey did not end with independence," Dr. Mwansa continued, his voice resolute. "It was merely the prologue to a saga of resilience, determination, and resilience."

With each word, he traced Zambia's evolution—from the heady days of nation-building to the tumultuous era of economic reform. "Through nationalization, diversification, and democratization, Zambia navigated the currents of change, charting a course towards a brighter future."

The students hung on his every word, their imaginations ablaze with visions of Zambia's past, present, and future. "And so," Dr. Mwansa declared, his voice ringing with conviction, "we stand on the shoulders of giants—inheritors of a legacy forged in the crucible of history, bound by the unbreakable spirit of Zambia's quest for development."

With a nod of reverence, he concluded, "But our journey has only just begun. For as scholars of developmental studies, it is our solemn duty to honor the sacrifices of the past, to learn from the lessons of history, and to forge a path forward—one of progress, prosperity, and promise."

And with that, the echoes of Zambia's past faded into the dusk, leaving behind a legacy of hope, resilience, and unyielding determination.

Key Concepts and Terminologies

As the evening shadows deepened, Dr. Mwansa's voice reverberated through the lecture hall, infusing the air with a sense of anticipation and intrigue.

"Now, my dear students," he began, his eyes alight with enthusiasm, "let us delve into the lexicon of development—the language that will guide our exploration of Zambia's developmental landscape."

With a flourish, he unfurled a scroll, its parchment weathered with age, adorned with the intricate symbols of academia. "Behold," he proclaimed, "the key concepts and terminologies that shall illuminate our path."

As the students leaned forward, their minds ablaze with curiosity, Dr. Mwansa began to unravel the mysteries of development. "At the heart of our discourse lies the concept of sustainable development—a delicate balance of economic growth, social equity, and environmental stewardship."

With each word, he painted a vivid tapestry of inter-connectedness, where prosperity intertwined with justice, and progress danced with sustainability. "From the pillars of human capital and social cohesion to the imperatives of governance and accountability, these concepts form the bedrock of our inquiry."

The students nodded in solemn recognition, their hearts quickening with understanding. "But let us not forget," Dr. Mwansa cautioned, his voice tinged with gravitas, "the nuances of our discourse—the subtle shades of meaning that shape our understanding."

With a deft motion, he pointed to the scroll, tracing the contours of words like empowerment, resilience, and in-clusivity. "These," he declared, "are not mere words, but guiding principles—beacons of light that illuminate the path to Zambia's development."

The students scribbled furiously, their quills scratching against parchment, capturing the wisdom that flowed from Dr. Mwansa's lips. "And so," he concluded, his voice ringing with conviction, "let us wield this knowledge with humility, empathy, and unwavering resolve—as stewards of Zambia's future, guardians of progress, and champions of hope."

With a final flourish, he rolled up the scroll, its secrets safely ensconced within its ancient folds. And as the students filed out into the night, their minds ablaze with newfound under-standing, they carried with them the torch of knowledge—the key to unlocking Zambia's boundless potential.

Importance of an Interdisciplinary Approach for Zambia

As the first stars began to twinkle in the evening sky, Dr. Mwansa stood before his captivated audience, the glow of determination illuminating his face. "Now, my scholars," he began, his voice echoing with purpose, "we must turn our attention to a cornerstone of our studies—the importance of an interdisciplinary approach for Zambia."

The students leaned forward, their curiosity piqued. Dr. Mwansa gestured toward a large, intricately detailed mural that spanned the length of the lecture hall. The mural depicted various scenes from Zambian life: bustling markets, vast agricultural fields, traditional ceremonies, and modern urban landscapes.

"Look around you," Dr. Mwansa urged, his voice soft yet compelling. "Zambia is a mosaic of interwoven lives, cultures, and ecosystems. To truly grasp the essence of our development, we cannot view it through a single lens."

He moved closer to the mural, pointing to a scene of farmers working the land. "Consider agriculture," he said. "To understand its role in our development, we must consider not just the economic factors, but also the environmental impact, the cultural practices, and the social dynamics at play."

Dr. Mwansa then walked to a depiction of a Zambian city, teeming with life and activity. "Urbanization," he continued. "It is not merely about building infrastructure. It's about planning for sustainable growth, ensuring social equity, fostering political stability, and preserving our cultural heritage."

The students nodded, beginning to see the intricate web of connections. "By integrating multiple disciplines," Dr. Mwansa explained, "we can create holistic solutions that address the complexities of our nation's challenges."

He paused, allowing his words to sink in. "An interdisciplinary approach enables us to see the full picture, to appreciate the interdependencies, and to innovate in ways that are both sustainable and inclusive."

Drawing back from the mural, he faced the students, his expression earnest. "In Zambia, where our history, culture, and natural resources are so deeply interconnected, an interdisciplinary approach is not just beneficial—it is essential."

With a sweeping gesture, he encompassed the entire mural, symbolizing the unity of diverse elements. "Our future depends on our ability to harness the knowledge from economics, sociology, politics, environmental science, and beyond. Only then can we forge a path that honors our past, embraces our present, and ensures a prosperous future for all."

The students, inspired by Dr. Mwansa's passion and clarity, felt the weight of their responsibility. They understood that their role was to weave these threads of knowledge into a cohesive tapestry, one that would support Zambia's ongoing development.

As they left the hall, the image of the mural lingered in their minds, a constant reminder of the intricate, interconnected journey they were about to undertake—guided by the interdisciplinary approach that Dr. Mwansa so passionately championed.

Major Theories in Developmental Studies with Zambian Examples

As the classroom settled into a reflective hush, the murmur of students exchanging ideas filled the air with a sense of eager anticipation. Dr. Mwansa stood at the front, his eyes scanning the eager faces before him. "Now, we turn our focus to the major theories in developmental studies," he began, his voice imbued with scholarly fervor. "These are the lenses through which we analyze, understand, and envision Zambia's path to progress."

He moved to a large chalkboard, its surface pristine and ready for the weighty concepts he was about to inscribe. "First, let us consider Modernization Theory," he said, chalk in hand. "This theory posits that development follows a linear progression from traditional to modern societies."

With swift strokes, he sketched the outline of a timeline, marking significant milestones. "For Zambia," he continued, "this can be seen in our transition from colonial rule to an independent state, striving for industrialization and modern infrastructure. Think of our ambitious projects like the TAZARA Railway—a symbol of progress and connectivity."

The students nodded, picturing the vast railway stretching across the African landscape, linking Zambia to new opportunities and growth.

Next, Dr. Mwansa wrote "Dependency Theory" in bold letters. "This theory challenges the notion of linear development, emphasizing how historical exploitation and unequal economic relations can trap countries like Zambia in a cycle of dependency."

He drew a web of interconnected lines, representing global

trade networks. "Consider our reliance on copper exports," he explained. "While this resource has fuelled our economy, it has also made us vulnerable to global market fluctuations. To break free from this dependency, we must diversify and strengthen other sectors."

A murmur of agreement rippled through the room as the students grasped the complexities of Zambia's economic dependencies.

Dr. Mwansa then turned to "World-Systems Theory," inscribing it with a flourish. "This theory views the world as a single social system, divided into core, semi-periphery, and periphery nations. Zambia, often seen as part of the periphery, provides raw materials to the industrialized core."

He illustrated this with a diagram of concentric circles. "However," he added, "Zambia has the potential to shift within this system by leveraging our natural resources, enhancing our human capital, and fostering regional cooperation within bodies like the Southern African Development Community (SADC)."

The students, eyes alight with curiosity, envisioned a Zambia that could rise within the global hierarchy, empowered by strategic alliances and innovative policies.

"Next, we delve into Postcolonial Theory," he announced, writing the term with deliberate precision. "This perspective examines the lasting impacts of colonialism on former colonies, urging us to reclaim our narratives and cultural identities."

Dr. Mwansa spoke passionately about Zambia's rich cultural heritage and the importance of integrating indigenous knowledge into development strategies. "Think of our traditional farming techniques and community-based conservation efforts," he said. "These are not relics of the past, but vital components of sustainable development."

A sense of pride and recognition filled the room as students reflected on the unique strengths of their cultural heritage.

Finally, Dr. Mwansa introduced "Human Development Theory," writing it with a sense of finality. "This theory focuses on expanding people's capabilities and opportunities, beyond mere economic growth."

He highlighted Zambia's efforts to improve education, healthcare, and gender equality. "The Human Development Index (HDI) measures our progress, but true development is seen in the lives improved, the dreams realized, and the potential unleashed."

The students, inspired by this holistic view, saw themselves as agents of change, committed to enhancing the quality of life for all Zambians.

As Dr. Mwansa stepped back from the chalkboard, now covered with the rich tapestry of theories and examples, he surveyed the room. "These theories provide us with different lenses to understand our journey. Each offers insights and challenges, guiding us toward a nuanced and comprehensive approach to development."

The classroom buzzed with excitement, the students ready to apply these theories to their own analyses and projects. They left the hall with a renewed sense of purpose, armed with the knowledge and inspiration to contribute to Zambia's ongoing development.

Dr. Mwansa watched them go, a smile playing on his lips, confident that these future leaders would carry forward the legacy of critical thought and interdisciplinary collaboration essential for Zambia's progress.

Contemporary Issues and Debates in Zambia

As dawn broke, casting a warm glow over the University of Zambia, students filled the lecture hall, buzzing with anticipation. Dr. Mwansa stood at the front, his demeanor serious yet invigorated by the day's topic.

"Today," he began, his voice resonating with urgency, "we confront the contemporary issues and debates that shape our nation's development. These are the pressing challenges and dynamic discussions that demand our attention and action."

He moved to a large screen at the front of the room, displaying images and headlines from recent Zambian news. "Our first issue," he said, pointing to an image of dry, cracked earth, "is climate change. Zambia, with its vast agricultural lands, is facing severe droughts and unpredictable weather patterns, threatening food security and livelihoods."

The students nodded, recognizing the impact on their communities. "Debates rage over the best path forward," Dr. Mwansa continued. "Should we invest heavily in irrigation and new farming techniques, or should we focus on diversifying our economy to reduce reliance on agriculture?"

A student raised her hand. "Both are crucial," she said. "But we must also consider community-based approaches that incorporate indigenous knowledge."

Dr. Mwansa smiled, pleased by her insight. "Exactly. We must balance innovation with tradition, ensuring sustainable and inclusive solutions."

Next, he highlighted an image of bustling city streets. "Urbanization presents another complex issue. As our cities grow, we face challenges in housing, infrastructure, and public services. Debates emerge about how to manage this growth sustainably."

He pointed to a map showing urban expansion in Lusaka. "Should we prioritize high-density housing to conserve space, or focus on expanding the city outward? Each choice has profound implications for our environment and social fabric."

Another student chimed in, "And what about informal settlements? We need policies that address their needs without marginalizing these communities."

Dr. Mwansa nodded, acknowledging the comment. "Indeed, inclusive urban planning is vital to ensure all citizens benefit from development."

He then shifted to an image of a classroom filled with eager students. "Education is our next critical issue. While we've made strides in increasing access, debates continue over the quality of education and its alignment with job market needs."

The screen displayed statistics on literacy rates and employment figures. "How do we reform our education system to better prepare our youth for the future? Should we focus on vocational training, higher education, or a blend of both?"

A student in the back raised his hand. "We need to integrate technology into our classrooms and curriculums, but also ensure that rural areas are not left behind."

"Precisely," Dr. Mwansa agreed. "Bridging the digital divide is essential for equitable development."

He moved to a final set of images showing women in leadership and advocacy roles. "Gender equality remains a contentious and vital issue. Despite progress, significant disparities persist in education, employment, and political representation."

The students saw images of protests and campaigns for women's rights. "Debates center on how best to achieve gender parity. Should we enforce quotas in politics and business, or focus on grassroots empowerment and education?"

A young woman in the front row spoke up, "We need both systemic change and cultural shifts. Empowering women at all levels will drive broader societal transformation."

Dr. Mwansa looked around the room, his gaze intense. "These contemporary issues and debates are not abstract; they are the realities we face daily. As scholars and future leaders, your role is to engage with these challenges, contribute to these debates, and work towards solutions that honor our heritage while embracing progress."

He paused, letting the gravity of his words settle over the room. "The path ahead is fraught with complexities, but it is also ripe with opportunities. Your insights, actions, and dedication will shape the future of Zambia."

As the students filed out, their minds racing with ideas and resolve, Dr. Mwansa felt a deep sense of hope. He knew that within this room were the voices that would steer Zambia through its contemporary challenges, crafting a future defined by thoughtful debate, inclusive solutions, and unwavering commitment to development.

2

Chapter 2: Theories of Development

Application of Modernization Theory in Zambia

As the afternoon sun cast long shadows across the University of Zambia's campus, students gathered once more in the lecture hall, their faces reflecting a mixture of curiosity and determination. Dr. Mwansa stood at the front, his demeanor energetic as he prepared to delve into the application of modernization theory in Zambia.

"Welcome back, scholars," he began, his voice full of enthusiasm. "Today, we explore how modernization theory has been applied within our nation—a theory that has profoundly influenced our development policies and aspirations."

He moved to a projector, which displayed a historical photo of Lusaka in the 1960s, a time when Zambia had just gained independence. "Modernization theory posits that societies progress through stages of development, moving from traditional to modern states," he explained. "When Zambia gained independence in 1964, we stood at the threshold of

14

this journey."

The image shifted to show the TAZARA Railway being constructed. "One of the most emblematic projects of our modernization efforts was the TAZARA Railway," Dr. Mwansa said, his eyes shining with pride. "This railway was more than just tracks and trains. It symbolized our leap towards industrialization and connectivity, linking us to the port of Dar es Salaam in Tanzania and opening up new trade routes."

He pointed to a graph depicting economic growth over the decades. "The early years post-independence saw significant investments in infrastructure, education, and health—key pillars of modernization theory. Our leaders believed that by building these foundations, we could transform Zambia into a modern, industrialized nation."

The screen then showed bustling images of Lusaka's markets and factories from the 1970s and 1980s. "However, modernization is not without its challenges," Dr. Mwansa continued. "While we saw initial growth, the global economic crises and falling copper prices of the 1970s and 1980s hit us hard. Our reliance on copper—a single commodity—exposed the vulnerabilities in our development strategy."

A student raised her hand. "Did the theory account for such external shocks?" she asked, her brow furrowed in concern.

"An excellent question," Dr. Mwansa responded. "Modernization theory, while optimistic, often overlooked the complexities and external dependencies faced by developing nations. Zambia's experience highlighted the need for a more diversified economy."

He then showed a modern image of Lusaka, with skyscrapers and bustling traffic. "Despite these setbacks, the principles of modernization continued to guide us. Recent decades have seen renewed efforts to diversify our economy, invest in technology, and improve governance. The establishment of the Lusaka Stock Exchange in 1994, for instance, was a step towards integrating our economy with global financial markets."

The projector then displayed images of new universities, hospitals, and technology hubs springing up across the country. "Education and health have remained at the forefront of our modernization efforts," he said. "Today, our universities are producing graduates equipped with the skills needed for a modern economy, and our health infrastructure is expanding to meet the needs of a growing population."

Dr. Mwansa paused, letting the weight of Zambia's journey sink in. "Modernization theory has provided a framework for our aspirations, but our experience has also taught us the importance of resilience, adaptability, and inclusivity. Our path is not a straight line but a dynamic process shaped by our unique context and challenges."

A student in the back raised his hand. "So, where do we go from here?" he asked, a note of determination in his voice.

Dr. Mwansa smiled, a hint of pride in his eyes. "We continue to build on the foundations laid by modernization theory, but with a nuanced approach that addresses our specific needs and circumstances. This means embracing innovation, fostering sustainable practices, and ensuring that all Zambians benefit from our progress."

As the lecture drew to a close, the students felt a renewed sense of purpose. They understood that the application of modernization theory in Zambia was more than a historical narrative—it was a living, evolving journey. They left the hall with a deeper appreciation of their nation's past efforts and a strong resolve to contribute to its future development.

Dr. Mwansa watched them go, confident that these future leaders would carry forward the lessons of modernization theory, applying them with the wisdom and insight needed to navigate the complexities of Zambia's continued development.

Impact of Dependency Theory on Zambia's Economy

As the lecture hall filled with the chatter of students settling into their seats, the atmosphere buzzed with anticipation. The day's topic promised to be both challenging and deeply relevant to their understanding of Zambia's economic landscape. Dr. Mwansa stood at the front, his presence commanding attention as he prepared to address the complex impact of dependency theory on Zambia's economy.

"Welcome, everyone," he began, his voice cutting through the noise. "Today, we explore the profound impact of dependency theory on our nation's economic journey."

He dimmed the lights, and the projector illuminated the screen with a map of Zambia and its rich natural resources, notably copper. "Dependency theory," he explained, "posits that developing nations, like Zambia, are often trapped in a cycle of dependence on more developed countries. This dependency is rooted in historical exploitation and continues through economic structures that favor the wealthier nations."

The image shifted to colonial-era photos of miners extracting copper. "During colonial rule, Zambia's economy was heavily oriented towards the extraction and export of raw materials, primarily copper. This set the stage for a dependent economic structure, where we supplied raw materials to industrialized nations, receiving finished goods in return."

Dr. Mwansa moved to a graph showing the fluctuating prices of copper over the decades. "After gaining independence, Zambia continued to rely on copper as its economic backbone. However, this dependence on a single commodity left us vulnerable to global market fluctuations. When copper prices fell, our economy suffered immensely."

The students watched intently as the screen displayed images of closed mines and abandoned machinery. "The economic downturns of the 1970s and 1980s were stark reminders of our vulnerability. Dependency theory helps us understand how external economic forces and our position in the global market can perpetuate cycles of poverty and underdevelopment."

A student raised his hand, his expression thoughtful. "So, how did this theory influence our policies?" he asked.

Dr. Mwansa smiled, appreciating the engagement. "Excellent question. Recognizing the pitfalls of dependency, Zambia's leaders began to advocate for diversification and self-reliance. Efforts were made to develop other sectors, such as agriculture and manufacturing, to reduce our dependence on copper."

He showed images of agricultural projects and local manufacturing plants. "Initiatives like the development of export crops, such as tobacco and sugar, and the establishment of local industries aimed to create a more resilient economy. However, these efforts faced significant challenges, including limited infrastructure, lack of capital, and competition from established global players."

The screen then displayed photos of international summits and regional meetings. "In the 1990s and 2000s, Zambia also sought to strengthen regional cooperation through organizations like the Southern African Development Community (SADC). By building stronger ties with our neighbors, we aimed to create a more balanced and interdependent regional economy, less susceptible to the whims of distant markets."

A student near the front raised her hand. "What about the role of international aid and foreign investment?" she asked.

"Another crucial aspect," Dr. Mwansa replied, nodding. "Dependency theory also critiques the role of international aid and foreign investment, arguing that these often come with strings attached, reinforcing dependency rather than fostering genuine development."

He displayed a diagram showing the flow of aid and investment. "While foreign aid and investment have brought much-needed resources, they can also perpetuate dependency if not managed wisely. It's vital to ensure that such engagements build local capacity and empower Zambians to drive their own development."

As the lecture continued, Dr. Mwansa spoke of the current efforts to navigate these complex dynamics. "Today, we are more aware of the need for economic sovereignty. By investing in education, technology, and sustainable practices, we strive to build an economy that is resilient and self-sustaining."

He ended with a hopeful note, showing images of young Zambian entrepreneurs and thriving local businesses. "The future lies in our ability to innovate and adapt, to learn from the past and create new pathways for development."

The students left the hall deep in thought, grappling with the realities of dependency and the challenges of breaking free from its constraints. They felt a renewed sense of responsibility to contribute to a future where Zambia could stand strong and independent in the global economy.

Dr. Mwansa watched them go, confident that these future leaders would carry forward the lessons of dependency theory, applying them with the insight and creativity needed to forge a resilient and prosperous Zambia.

World-Systems Theory and Zambia's Position

The afternoon sun filtered through the tall windows of the lecture hall, casting a warm glow on the eager faces of the students. Dr. Mwansa stood at the front, a map of the world projected behind him, its lines and colors stark against the white screen. Today's lecture promised to delve into the intricacies of World-Systems Theory and Zambia's place within this global framework.

"Good afternoon, everyone," he began, his voice steady and engaging. "Today, we tackle World-Systems Theory, a perspective that helps us understand the global economic order and Zambia's position within it."

He gestured towards the map, which highlighted different regions in varying shades of color. "World-Systems Theory, developed by sociologist Immanuel Wallerstein, divides the world into three categories: the core, the semi-periphery, and the periphery. Core countries are highly industrialized, economically diversified, and wield significant global influence. Semi-peripheral countries are more developed than peripheral ones but still lack the full economic power of core nations. Peripheral countries, like Zambia, are often dependent on exporting raw materials and have less economic power."

The map zoomed in on Zambia, marked clearly in the periphery. "Zambia's historical and economic context places it firmly in the periphery. Our reliance on copper exports and the challenges of diversification are key aspects of this positioning."

He switched to a slide showing historical data on Zambia's copper production and export markets. "For decades, our economy has been heavily dependent on copper. This reliance ties us into a global economic system where we supply raw materials to more industrialized nations, which then process these materials into high-value goods."

A student raised her hand, curiosity in her eyes. "But how do we move up from the periphery? Is it possible for Zambia to become a semi-peripheral or even a core country?"

Dr. Mwansa smiled, appreciating the thoughtful question. "That's a critical question. Moving up in the global hierarchy is challenging but not impossible. It requires strategic efforts to diversify our economy, invest in education and technology, and build stronger regional and global partnerships."

He showed images of new industries emerging in Zambia, from agricultural processing plants to technology startups. "We are seeing efforts to diversify. For example, the development of the agricultural sector beyond subsistence farming to include cash crops like tobacco and coffee. Additionally, the rise of local tech startups signals a move towards a knowledge-based economy."

The screen then displayed photos of regional summits and international trade agreements. "Building regional alliances is another strategy. By strengthening economic ties within the Southern African Development Community (SADC), we can create a more integrated and robust regional economy that can negotiate better terms in the global market."

Another student interjected, "But doesn't this also depend on global economic conditions and the policies of core countries?"

"Absolutely," Dr. Mwansa agreed. "World-Systems Theory highlights that the global economic system is interconnected and often skewed to benefit the core countries. Therefore, while Zambia must work on internal strategies, we also need to engage in global advocacy for fairer trade practices and economic policies."

He displayed a final slide showing young Zambian entrepreneurs and innovative projects. "The path forward lies in leveraging our unique strengths and resources, fostering innovation, and ensuring that our development is inclusive and sustainable. Education and human capital development are crucial. By investing in our people, we build a workforce capable of driving economic transformation."

As the lecture concluded, Dr. Mwansa's voice took on a hopeful tone. "World-Systems Theory provides a lens to understand our challenges and our potential. Zambia's position in the global economic order is not fixed; it can change through strategic actions and collective effort."

The students left the hall, their minds buzzing with the complexities and possibilities of World-Systems Theory. They understood that while the path to economic advancement was fraught with challenges, it was also filled with opportunities for innovation, collaboration, and growth.

Dr. Mwansa watched them go, filled with confidence that these future leaders would navigate Zambia's place in the world with insight and determination, pushing the boundaries of the periphery towards a more influential and self-reliant position in the global system.

Postcolonial Perspectives on Zambian Development

The classroom was quiet, the air filled with anticipation. Students at the University of Zambia leaned forward, ready for the day's lecture on postcolonial perspectives and their impact on Zambia's development. Dr. Mwansa, always a captivating presence, stood at the front with a thoughtful expression.

"Good afternoon, everyone," he began, his voice rich with depth. "Today, we delve into postcolonial perspectives on our development journey—a critical lens that reveals how our colonial past continues to shape our present and future."

He clicked a button, and the screen lit up with a historical photograph of Zambia during the colonial era. "Colonial rule imposed artificial borders, disrupted indigenous governance systems, and reoriented our economy towards the needs of the colonial powers. Postcolonial theory helps us understand the lingering effects of these disruptions."

The image shifted to a modern view of Lusaka, juxtaposed against the colonial past. "Independence in 1964 marked a new beginning, yet the legacy of colonialism persisted. Our task has been to reclaim and redefine our identity, governance, and economic policies in a way that reflects our values and aspirations."

A student raised his hand. "Can you give us an example of how colonial legacies affect us today?"

"Absolutely," Dr. Mwansa responded, his eyes scanning the room. "Let's consider land ownership. During colonial times, vast tracts of fertile land were appropriated by colonial settlers, leaving indigenous populations with less productive land. Post-independence, redistributing this land has been fraught with legal and social challenges, impacting agricultural productivity and rural development."

The screen displayed a map highlighting regions with land ownership disputes. "Efforts to rectify these imbalances often meet resistance, reflecting the deep-seated issues rooted in our colonial past. The struggle for land justice is a vivid example of postcolonial challenges."

He then showed a video clip of a traditional ceremony, vibrant with dance and music. "Cultural reclamation is another crucial aspect. Colonial rule attempted to suppress our cultural expressions, imposing foreign values and systems. Postcolonialism emphasizes the importance of reviving and integrating indigenous cultures into our national identity and development strategies."

A student in the back raised her hand. "How does this cultural aspect tie into our economic and political development?"

"Excellent question," Dr. Mwansa said, smiling. "Our cultural heritage is a source of resilience and innovation. Integrating indigenous knowledge systems into areas like agriculture, medicine, and governance can lead to more sustainable and locally relevant development practices."

He displayed images of community-led projects that successfully combined modern and traditional practices. "For example, community-based conservation efforts often draw on indigenous knowledge of the land, leading to more effective and sustainable outcomes than externally imposed solutions."

The screen then shifted to a graph showing economic dependency patterns. "Postcolonial perspectives also critique our continued economic dependency on former colonial powers. While we have diversified our trade partners, the structures of global trade often perpetuate inequalities established during colonial times."

He paused, letting the gravity of these insights sink in. "Understanding these dynamics is essential for crafting policies that genuinely address our development needs. It means questioning whose interests are served by our economic policies and striving to create systems that benefit the majority of Zambians."

A student near the front spoke up, "So, how do we move forward from here? How do we break free from these postcolonial constraints?"

Dr. Mwansa's face lit up with a mix of challenge and hope. "Moving forward requires a multifaceted approach. It means embracing our cultural identity, promoting inclusive governance, and advocating for fairer global trade practices. Education plays a critical role in empowering the next generation to think critically and act boldly."

He ended with a powerful image of Zambian youth engaged in various development projects. "The future is in your hands. By understanding and addressing the legacies of colonialism, you can forge a path that honors our past while boldly shaping our future."

As the students left the hall, they carried with them a deeper understanding of the complexities of Zambia's development. They felt a renewed sense of purpose and responsibility to address the postcolonial challenges that continued to influence their nation's trajectory.

Dr. Mwansa watched them go, confident that these emerging leaders would navigate the postcolonial landscape with wisdom and determination, carving out a brighter, more equitable future for Zambia.

Human Development Theory: Zambian Indicators and Progress

The lecture hall at the University of Zambia was filled with an eager sense of curiosity as students settled into their seats. Today, Dr. Mwansa was set to discuss Human Development Theory, a topic that resonated deeply with their aspirations for a better Zambia.

"Good afternoon, everyone," Dr. Mwansa began, his voice carrying a warm, inviting tone. "Today, we'll explore Human Development Theory and how it applies to our beloved Zambia, focusing on key indicators and the progress we've made."

He displayed an image of the Human Development Index (HDI) components on the screen: health, education, and income. "Human Development Theory, championed by Amartya Sen and the United Nations Development Programme (UNDP), emphasizes that development is not just about economic growth but about improving people's well-being. The HDI is a composite measure that captures this holistic view."

The screen shifted to a graph showing Zambia's HDI trends over the past few decades. "Let's start with health," Dr. Mwansa said, highlighting the life expectancy line. "In the 1990s, Zambia's life expectancy was severely impacted by the HIV/AIDS epidemic. However, with international aid and robust health policies, we've seen significant improvements."

He displayed images of health clinics and community health workers. "The introduction of antiretroviral therapy (ART) and widespread health campaigns have been pivotal. Organizations like the Zambia National AIDS Network have played a crucial role in reducing the spread of HIV and improving the health of those affected."

A student raised her hand. "What about education?" she asked, her voice reflecting the importance of this topic to her personally.

"Excellent question," Dr. Mwansa replied, shifting to a slide showing school enrollment rates. "Education is another critical component of human development. In the past two decades, Zambia has made strides in increasing access to primary education, thanks to policies like the free basic education policy introduced in 2002."

The screen showed children in classrooms, their faces bright with the promise of learning. "Our challenge now is to improve the quality of education and ensure that higher levels of education are accessible to all. Initiatives like the Building Learning Foundations program aim to enhance literacy and numeracy skills, setting a strong foundation for lifelong learning."

He then displayed data on income and poverty reduction. "Economic opportunities are crucial for human development. While Zambia has seen some economic growth, especially in urban areas, rural poverty remains a significant challenge."

The screen showed images of rural development projects, from sustainable farming initiatives to microfinance programs. "Projects like the Rural Electrification Authority's efforts to provide electricity and the Citizen Economic Empowerment Commission's support for small businesses are vital in bridging the urban-rural divide."

A student in the back raised his hand. "How do these improvements in HDI translate to real-life impacts for Zambians?"

"Great question," Dr. Mwansa said, smiling. "Human Development Theory reminds us that development is about expanding people's freedoms and opportunities. Improvements in health mean that people can live longer, healthier lives. Better education opens up opportunities for employment and personal growth. Increased incomes allow families to improve their living standards and invest in their future."

He then shared a short video clip featuring a success story: a woman named Chanda, who had benefited from a microfinance program to start her own tailoring business. "Chanda's story is a testament to the power of human development. With access to health services, education, and economic opportunities, she's not only transformed her own life but also contributes to her community's development."

The lecture concluded with a hopeful image of Zambian children playing and learning. "The journey of human development is ongoing," Dr. Mwansa said, his voice filled with determination. "While we celebrate our progress, we must also recognize the work ahead. By focusing on health, education, and economic opportunities, we can continue to improve the well-being of all Zambians."

As the students left the hall, they felt a renewed sense of purpose. The principles of Human Development Theory had come alive for them, not just as abstract concepts, but as tangible goals for their country's future.

Dr. Mwansa watched them go, confident that these future leaders would carry forward the lessons of human development, striving to create a Zambia where every individual has the opportunity to thrive.

Sustainable Development Paradigms in Zambian Policy

The lecture hall was bathed in the warm glow of the afternoon sun. Dr. Mwansa stood at the front, ready to delve into the crucial topic of sustainable development. The students were keenly aware of the importance of this discussion for Zambia's future.

"Good afternoon, everyone," Dr. Mwansa began, his voice filled with a blend of urgency and hope. "Today, we explore sustainable development paradigms and their integration into Zambian policy."

He displayed an image of Zambia's lush landscapes and abundant natural resources. "Sustainable development seeks to balance economic growth, social inclusion, and environmental protection. In Zambia, this paradigm is essential for ensuring that our development is equitable and long-lasting."

The screen shifted to show Zambia's Vision 2030, a strategic plan aimed at transforming Zambia into a prosperous middle-income nation by 2030. "Our Vision 2030 is anchored in sustainability. It emphasizes diversified economic growth, improved social welfare, and environmental stewardship."

A student raised her hand. "Can you give us specific examples of sustainable policies?"

"Of course," Dr. Mwansa replied, transitioning to a slide showcasing various initiatives. "One key area is agriculture. Programs promoting conservation farming techniques help preserve soil health and increase yields sustainably. This reduces reliance on chemical fertilizers and pesticides, benefiting both the environment and farmers."

He then highlighted the use of renewable energy. "Zambia is investing in hydroelectric power and exploring solar energy.

Projects like the Scaling Solar initiative aim to increase the share of renewable energy in our grid, reducing carbon emissions and ensuring energy security."

The screen showed a map of protected areas. "Environmental conservation is another critical aspect. The establishment of national parks and wildlife reserves not only preserves biodiversity but also supports eco-tourism, creating jobs and promoting environmental awareness."

A student at the back raised his hand. "How does sustainable development address social issues?"

"Sustainable development is inherently social," Dr. Mwansa responded. "Policies like the Social Cash Transfer Program provide financial support to vulnerable households, reducing poverty and improving health and education outcomes. Moreover, promoting gender equality and women's empowerment is central to our sustainability goals."

He concluded with an image of community-led development projects. "The most effective sustainable development policies are those that engage communities. By involving local stakeholders in decision-making, we ensure that policies are relevant, accepted, and implemented successfully."

As the students left, they felt inspired by the tangible examples of sustainable development in their country. They understood that achieving sustainability was not just a governmental responsibility but a collective endeavor involving every citizen.

3

Chapter 3: Economic Development

Measuring Economic Growth in Zambia

The next lecture focused on the vital subject of economic growth measurement. The students entered the hall, aware that understanding these metrics was key to evaluating Zambia's progress.

"Good afternoon, everyone," Dr. Mwansa greeted, his tone serious and analytical. "Today, we focus on how we measure economic growth in Zambia and what these measurements reveal about our development."

He displayed a graph illustrating Zambia's GDP growth over the years. "Gross Domestic Product, or GDP, is the most common measure of economic growth. It represents the total value of goods and services produced within our borders."

The screen then showed various sectors contributing to GDP, such as mining, agriculture, and services. "Our economy is diverse, with significant contributions from mining, particularly copper, agriculture, and increasingly, the service sector."

A student raised her hand. "But GDP doesn't tell the whole story, right?"

"Correct," Dr. Mwansa acknowledged, nodding. "While GDP is important, it doesn't capture income distribution, poverty levels, or the quality of life. That's why we also look at other indicators like Gross National Income (GNI) and the Human Development Index (HDI)."

He transitioned to a slide showing GNI per capita. "GNI includes the income earned by Zambians abroad and provides a broader picture of national wealth. Increases in GNI can indicate improved economic well-being."

Next, he highlighted Zambia's HDI trends. "The HDI combines indicators of life expectancy, education, and income. It offers a more comprehensive view of development by reflecting health and educational outcomes alongside economic growth."

A student near the front raised his hand. "What about measuring poverty and inequality?"

"Excellent point," Dr. Mwansa said, bringing up data on poverty rates and the Gini coefficient. "Poverty rates show the percentage of the population living below the poverty line. The Gini coefficient measures income inequality, with 0 representing perfect equality and 1 representing extreme inequality."

He showed a map highlighting regions with high poverty levels. "In Zambia, rural areas often have higher poverty rates. Addressing these disparities is crucial for inclusive growth."

The screen then displayed charts of employment data and sectoral growth. "Employment rates and job creation are also vital indicators. Economic growth must translate into job opportunities and improved livelihoods for it to be meaningful."

He concluded with a thought-provoking image of a bustling market and a thriving industrial area. "Ultimately, measuring economic growth is about more than numbers. It's about understanding how these metrics impact the lives of Zambians. By using a variety of indicators, we can get a clearer picture of our progress and the areas needing attention."

As the students filed out, they reflected on the complexity of measuring economic growth. They appreciated that these metrics were not just academic but deeply connected to the well-being and prosperity of their nation.

Dr. Mwansa watched them leave, hopeful that this new generation would use these insights to drive forward Zambia's economic development with a nuanced and holistic approach.

Zambia's Development Indicators (GDP, GNI, HDI)

The lecture hall buzzed with the low murmur of students discussing the morning's topic. Dr. Mwansa stood at the front, ready to dive into the specifics of Zambia's development indicators: GDP, GNI, and HDI. He knew these metrics were crucial for understanding the nation's progress and challenges.

"Good afternoon, everyone," he began, his voice clear and engaging. "Today, we will delve into the key development indicators that help us gauge Zambia's progress: Gross Domestic Product (GDP), Gross National Income (GNI), and the Human Development Index (HDI)."

He clicked a button, and the first slide displayed a chart of Zambia's GDP growth over the past two decades. "GDP measures the total value of all goods and services produced within a country in a given year. It's a primary indicator of economic health and growth."

The chart showed peaks and valleys, reflecting periods of economic boom and slowdown. "In Zambia, our GDP has been significantly influenced by the mining sector, particularly copper. However, reliance on a single commodity can make us vulnerable to global price fluctuations."

He then displayed a map of Zambia with regions color-coded by economic activity. "While mining remains a cornerstone, we've seen growth in agriculture and services. Diversification is key to stabilizing our GDP and reducing economic volatility."

A student raised her hand. "How does GNI differ from GDP?"

"Great question," Dr. Mwansa said, switching to a slide showing GNI per capita. "GNI includes GDP plus net income from abroad, such as remittances and foreign investments. It gives a broader picture of the economic activity and resources available to the population."

He showed a comparative graph of GDP and GNI over several years. "GNI can be higher or lower than GDP, depending on whether a country is a net receiver or sender of income from abroad. For Zambia, GNI has generally tracked closely with GDP, reflecting our integrated yet domestically focused economy."

Next, he moved to a slide showing Zambia's HDI trends. "The Human Development Index combines life expectancy, education, and per capita income indicators to provide a more holistic measure of development."

The graph showed a steady upward trend, but with room for improvement. "Our HDI has improved over the years, but we still face challenges in health and education. Life expectancy has increased due to better healthcare, and educational attainment has improved with policies promoting access to schooling."

He displayed images of healthcare clinics and schools. "Investments in healthcare infrastructure and educational facilities are crucial. Programs targeting maternal and child health, as well as initiatives to improve literacy and vocational skills, directly contribute to our HDI."

A student near the front raised his hand. "What specific challenges do we face in improving our HDI further?"

"Excellent question," Dr. Mwansa replied, transitioning to a slide listing key challenges. "Poverty and inequality remain significant barriers. While we've made progress, many Zambians, particularly in rural areas, still lack access to quality healthcare and education."

He showed data on rural-urban disparities. "These disparities are evident in our HDI sub-indicators. Rural areas often have lower life expectancy and educational outcomes compared to urban centers. Addressing these gaps is essential for equitable development."

The final slide displayed a hopeful image of Zambian children in a classroom and farmers in a field. "Improving our development indicators requires a multifaceted approach: diversifying the economy, investing in health and education, and ensuring that growth benefits all Zambians."

As the students left the hall, they felt a deeper understanding of how GDP, GNI, and HDI interconnect to paint a comprehensive picture of Zambia's development. They realized that behind each statistic were real lives and stories of progress and struggle.

Dr. Mwansa watched them go, confident that these future leaders would leverage this knowledge to drive forward Zambia's development with empathy, insight, and a commitment to inclusive growth.

Impact of Globalization and Trade-in Zambia

The lecture hall was abuzz with anticipation as students settled into their seats, eager to learn about the impact of globalization and trade on Zambia's economic development. Dr. Mwansa stood at the front, a map of the world projected behind him, ready to delve into the complexities of this topic.

"Good afternoon, everyone," he greeted, his voice carrying a tone of authority tempered with warmth. "Today, we explore the profound influence of globalization and trade on Zambia's economic landscape."

He clicked a button, and the screen illuminated with images of bustling ports and cargo ships. "Globalization refers to the interconnectedness of economies and societies worldwide. For Zambia, globalization has opened up new opportunities for trade and investment, but it has also presented challenges."

The next slide displayed graphs showing Zambia's trade patterns over the years. "Trade plays a significant role in our economy. We export commodities like copper, cobalt, and agricultural products, while importing manufactured goods and machinery."

A student raised her hand. "How does trade benefit Zambia?"

"Trade stimulates economic growth by allowing us to specialize in producing goods and services where we have a comparative advantage," Dr. Mwansa explained. "For example, Zambia's abundant mineral resources make us a leading exporter of copper, contributing to foreign exchange earnings and government revenue."

He then displayed a chart showing the composition of Zambia's exports and imports. "However, our reliance on a few primary commodities makes us vulnerable to fluctuations in global commodity prices. Diversifying our exports and enhancing value addition are critical for building resilience against external shocks."

The screen shifted to show images of industrial zones and trade agreements. "Globalization has also facilitated foreign direct investment (FDI) in Zambia, particularly in sectors like mining, manufacturing, and infrastructure. FDI brings in capital, technology, and expertise, stimulating job creation and industrial development."

A student in the back raised his hand. "What are the downsides of globalization and trade for Zambia?"

"An insightful question," Dr. Mwansa acknowledged, bringing up a slide listing challenges. "Globalization can exacerbate inequalities and erode local industries. For example, cheap imports can undercut domestic producers, leading to job losses and industrial decline."

He showed images of protests against trade liberalization policies. "Trade liberalization, while promoting efficiency and competitiveness, can also pose challenges for vulnerable groups like smallholder farmers and workers in sunset industries. It's essential to have policies in place to cushion the impacts and ensure that trade benefits are equitably distributed."

He then displayed a graph showing Zambia's trade balance over the years. "Maintaining a favorable trade balance is crucial for sustainable development. While we've seen improvements in recent years, reducing trade deficits requires enhancing productivity, promoting value addition, and fostering export-oriented industries."

As the lecture concluded, Dr. Mwansa left the students with a final thought. "Globalization and trade are powerful forces shaping Zambia's economic future. By embracing opportunities and addressing challenges, we can harness the benefits of globalization while safeguarding our national interests and promoting inclusive growth."

The students left the hall, their minds swirling with newfound insights into the complexities of globalization and trade. They understood that while these forces presented both opportunities and challenges, the key lay in navigating them with wisdom and foresight.

Dr. Mwansa watched them go, confident that they would carry forward the lessons learned in the lecture hall, equipped to contribute meaningfully to Zambia's economic development in an increasingly interconnected world.

Industrialization and Urbanization in Zambian Context

The lecture hall was alive with energy as students eagerly awaited the next topic in their exploration of economic development in Zambia. Dr. Mwansa stood at the front, a map of Zambia projected behind him, ready to delve into the intricate relationship between industrialization and urbanization.

"Good afternoon, everyone," he greeted, his voice resonating with enthusiasm. "Today, we embark on a journey to understand how industrialization and urbanization shape Zambia's economic landscape."

He clicked a button, and the screen illuminated with images of bustling cities and factories. "Industrialization refers to the process of transforming an economy from primarily agrarian to one based on manufacturing and services. Urbanization, on the other hand, involves the migration of people from rural areas to cities in search of economic opportunities."

The next slide displayed graphs showing the growth of Zambia's industrial sector over the years. "Industrialization is crucial for economic diversification and job creation. In Zambia, industries such as mining, manufacturing, and construction play a significant role in driving economic growth."

A student raised her hand. "How does industrialization contribute to urbanization?"

"An excellent question," Dr. Mwansa replied, bringing up a slide showing urbanization trends. "Industrialization creates employment opportunities in urban centers, attracting rural migrants seeking better livelihoods. As industries expand, so do cities, leading to urban growth and development."

He then displayed images of industrial zones and urban infrastructure. "However, rapid urbanization also poses challenges such as inadequate housing, congestion, and environmental degradation. It's essential for policymakers to plan and manage urban growth effectively to ensure sustainable development."

A student in the front row raised his hand. "How can industrialization benefit rural areas?"

"Another insightful question," Dr. Mwansa said, nodding appreciatively. "Industrialization can promote rural development by creating linkages between urban industries and rural suppliers. For example, agro-processing industries can add value to agricultural products, creating markets for smallholder farmers and boosting rural incomes."

He then displayed a graph showing the distribution of industries across Zambia. "Moreover, promoting industrial development in rural areas can alleviate pressure on urban centers and reduce rural-urban disparities. Initiatives like the Industrial Development Corporation's support for rural enterprises are vital in this regard."

As the lecture concluded, Dr. Mwansa left the students with a final thought. "Industrialization and urbanization are two sides of the same coin, driving Zambia's economic transformation. By harnessing the opportunities, they present and addressing the challenges they pose, we can create a more prosperous and equitable future for all Zambians."

The students left the hall, their minds buzzing with new-found insights into the dynamic interplay between industrialization and urbanization. They understood that by embracing these processes responsibly, Zambia could pave the way for sustainable development and inclusive growth.

Dr. Mwansa watched them go, confident that they would carry forward the lessons learned in the lecture hall, ready to contribute to Zambia's economic development with creativity, resilience, and foresight.

Addressing Poverty and Inequality in Zambia

The lecture hall was filled with a palpable sense of anticipation as students prepared to delve into the critical topic of poverty and inequality in Zambia. Dr. Mwansa stood at the front, his demeanor serious yet determined, ready to guide his students through this complex and pressing issue.

"Good afternoon, everyone," he began, his voice commanding attention. "Today, we confront one of the most urgent challenges facing our nation: poverty and inequality."

He clicked a button, and the screen illuminated with images depicting the stark realities of poverty in Zambia: dilapidated homes, crowded slums, and faces marked by hardship. "Poverty is a harsh reality for millions of Zambians, depriving them of basic necessities and opportunities for a better life."

The next slide displayed graphs showing income distribution patterns and poverty rates across different regions of Zambia. "Income inequality exacerbates poverty, with wealth concentrated in the hands of a few while the majority struggle to make ends meet."

A student raised her hand. "How does poverty affect different segments of the population?"

"An important question," Dr. Mwansa acknowledged, bringing up a slide highlighting vulnerable groups. "Women, children, and rural communities are disproportionately affected by poverty. Limited access to education, healthcare, and economic opportunities perpetuates the cycle of poverty for these groups."

He then displayed images of community-led initiatives and social programs. "Addressing poverty requires a multifaceted approach. Social protection programs, such as cash transfers and food assistance, provide immediate relief to the most vulnerable while promoting their long-term well-being."

A student in the back row raised his hand. "What role can economic policies play in reducing poverty and inequality?"

"Economic policies play a crucial role," Dr. Mwansa replied, transitioning to a slide showing policy interventions. "Pro-poor policies that promote inclusive growth, such as investing in education, healthcare, and rural infrastructure, can help lift people out of poverty and reduce inequality."

He then displayed a graph showing the impact of policy interventions on poverty rates. "Evidence-based policymaking is essential for targeting resources where they are needed most and evaluating the effectiveness of interventions over time."

As the lecture concluded, Dr. Mwansa left the students with a final thought. "Poverty and inequality are not insurmountable challenges. With political will, collective action, and a commitment to social justice, we can build a Zambia where every citizen has the opportunity to thrive."

The students left the hall, their hearts heavy with the weight of the issues discussed, but also filled with a newfound determination to be part of the solution. They understood that combating poverty and inequality required more than just words—it demanded action, solidarity, and empathy.

Dr. Mwansa watched them go, his faith in their ability to effect change unwavering. He knew that with their passion and dedication, they would be the architects of a more just and equitable Zambia.

Policy Interventions for Economic Growth in Zambia

The lecture hall was filled with anticipation as Dr. Mwansa prepared to discuss policy interventions for economic growth in Zambia. The students, eager to learn how their country could prosper, leaned forward in their seats, ready to absorb every word.

"Good afternoon, everyone," Dr. Mwansa began, his voice resonating with authority and enthusiasm. "Today, we explore the policy interventions that can drive economic growth and development in Zambia."

He clicked a button, and the screen illuminated with images of policymakers and economists discussing strategies for economic advancement. "Policy interventions are essential tools in shaping the trajectory of our economy and improving the lives of our people."

The next slide displayed graphs showing the impact of various policies on economic indicators such as GDP growth, inflation, and unemployment. "Investing in infrastructure is a cornerstone of economic development," Dr. Mwansa explained. "Improving roads, bridges, and energy systems enhances productivity, facilitates trade, and attracts investment."

A student raised her hand. "How can we ensure that infrastructure investments benefit all Zambians?"

"An excellent question," Dr. Mwansa replied, bringing up a slide highlighting inclusive infrastructure development. "Infrastructure projects should prioritize underserved areas, such as rural communities, and incorporate sustainable practices to minimize environmental impacts. Moreover, involving local communities in the planning and implementation process ensures that projects meet their needs and aspirations."

He then displayed images of entrepreneurship and innovation hubs. "Promoting entrepreneurship and innovation is another key policy intervention. Supporting small and medium-sized enterprises (SMEs) fosters job creation, fosters innovation, and diversifies the economy beyond traditional sectors."

A student in the front row raised his hand. "What role can trade policies play in stimulating economic growth?"

"Trade policies are vital," Dr. Mwansa replied, transitioning to a slide showing trade agreements and export promotion initiatives. "Facilitating trade through agreements with other countries opens up new markets for Zambian goods and services, driving export-led growth. Moreover, reducing trade barriers and streamlining customs procedures enhances the competitiveness of our exports."

He then displayed a graph showing the impact of export promotion programs on trade volumes. "Export diversification is crucial for resilience against external shocks. By supporting value addition and promoting non-traditional exports, we can reduce dependence on a few commodities and strengthen our economic resilience."

As the lecture concluded, Dr. Mwansa left the students with a final thought. "Policy interventions are powerful tools for shaping our economic future. By pursuing inclusive and sustainable policies, we can create an economy that works for all Zambians, fostering prosperity, resilience, and shared prosperity."

The students left the hall, their minds buzzing with ideas and possibilities. They understood that the policies discussed were not just theoretical concepts but practical tools for transforming Zambia's economy and improving the lives of its people.

Dr. Mwansa watched them go, filled with hope and optimism for the future. He knew that with their passion and dedication, they would be the architects of Zambia's economic success, driving forward policies that would pave the way for a brighter tomorrow.

4

Chapter 4: Social Development

Education and Human Capital in Zambia

The lecture hall was alive with anticipation as Dr. Mwansa prepared to delve into the crucial topic of education and human capital development in Zambia. The students, eager to understand the role of education in shaping the nation's future, listened intently, their eyes fixed on the professor at the front of the room.

"Good afternoon, everyone," Dr. Mwansa greeted, his voice filled with warmth and authority. "Today, we embark on a journey to explore the pivotal role of education in fostering human capital development in Zambia."

He clicked a button, and the screen illuminated with images of classrooms, students, and teachers engaged in the learning process. "Education is the cornerstone of development. It equips individuals with the knowledge, skills, and capabilities needed to thrive in an ever-changing world."

The next slide displayed graphs showing education indicators such as enrollment rates, literacy rates, and educational attainment levels across different regions of Zambia. "While significant progress has been made in expanding access to education, challenges remain," Dr. Mwansa explained. "Disparities in access, quality, and outcomes persist, particularly in rural and marginalized communities."

A student raised her hand. "How can we ensure that education is inclusive and equitable for all Zambians?"

"An excellent question," Dr. Mwansa replied, bringing up a slide highlighting inclusive education policies. "Inclusive education policies aim to remove barriers to access and participation for marginalized groups, such as girls, children with disabilities, and those living in remote areas. This includes providing targeted support, such as scholarships, transportation assistance, and accessible learning materials."

He then displayed images of well-equipped classrooms and qualified teachers. "Investing in quality education is essential," Dr. Mwansa emphasized. "This includes recruiting and training qualified teachers, improving infrastructure and learning materials, and adopting innovative teaching methods that cater to diverse learning needs."

A student in the back row raised his hand. "How does education contribute to human capital development and economic growth?"

"Education is a catalyst for human capital development," Dr. Mwansa replied, transitioning to a slide showing the link between education and economic productivity. "By equipping individuals with the skills and knowledge needed to succeed in the workforce, education enhances productivity, fosters innovation, and drives economic growth."

He then displayed graphs showing the impact of education

on employment rates and earnings. "Moreover, education is associated with better health outcomes, higher incomes, and greater social mobility. Investing in education, therefore, not only benefits individuals but also society as a whole."

As the lecture concluded, Dr. Mwansa left the students with a final thought. "Education is not just a fundamental human right; it is also a powerful driver of development. By ensuring inclusive, quality education for all Zambians, we can unlock their full potential and build a more prosperous and equitable society."

The students left the hall, their minds buzzing with new-found insights into the transformative power of education. They understood that by investing in education, Zambia could unlock a brighter future for generations to come.

Dr. Mwansa watched them go, filled with optimism for the impact they would make as future leaders and change-makers in their country. He knew that with their passion and dedication, they would continue to champion education as a cornerstone of Zambia's development journey.

Health and Well-Being: Zambian Perspectives

The lecture hall hummed with anticipation as Dr. Mwansa prepared to explore the critical topic of health and well-being in Zambia. The students, keenly aware of the importance of health in shaping individuals and communities, leaned forward in their seats, eager to learn from their esteemed professor.

"Good afternoon, everyone," Dr. Mwansa greeted, his voice carrying a tone of empathy and determination. "Today, we turn our attention to the essential role of health and well-being in the lives of Zambians."

He clicked a button, and the screen illuminated with images of healthcare facilities, medical professionals, and communities coming together to promote health. "Health is not merely the absence of disease but a state of physical, mental, and social well-being," Dr. Mwansa explained. "It is a fundamental human right and a cornerstone of development."

The next slide displayed graphs showing health indicators such as life expectancy, infant mortality rates, and disease prevalence across different regions of Zambia. "While significant progress has been made in improving health outcomes, challenges persist," Dr. Mwansa continued. "Access to quality healthcare, especially in rural and underserved areas, remains a concern."

A student raised her hand. "How can we address the disparities in access to healthcare in Zambia?"

"An excellent question," Dr. Mwansa replied, bringing up a slide highlighting strategies for improving healthcare access. "One approach is to strengthen primary healthcare systems, which serve as the first point of contact for individuals seeking healthcare services. This includes investing in infrastructure, training healthcare workers, and ensuring the availability of essential medicines and supplies."

He then displayed images of community health workers conducting outreach activities. "Community-based health initiatives play a crucial role in reaching underserved populations," Dr. Mwansa emphasized. "By engaging communities in health promotion and disease prevention efforts, we can improve health outcomes and reduce disparities."

A student in the front row raised his hand. "How can we address the social determinants of health, such as poverty and education?"

"Addressing the social determinants of health requires a multi-sectoral approach," Dr. Mwansa replied, transitioning to a slide showing the interconnected nature of health and social factors. "Policies that promote economic development, education, gender equality, and social protection can have significant impacts on health outcomes. By addressing underlying social inequities, we can create conditions that support health and well-being for all."

He then displayed graphs showing the impact of social determinants on health outcomes. "Moreover, investing in preventive healthcare measures, such as immunizations, maternal and child health services, and health education, can help reduce the burden of disease and improve overall health."

As the lecture concluded, Dr. Mwansa left the students with a final thought. "Health is a foundation for human development and a prerequisite for achieving our full potential. By working together to address the social, economic, and environmental factors that influence health, we can create a healthier and more prosperous Zambia for all."

The students left the hall, their minds buzzing with new-found insights into the complexities of health and well-being. They understood that by prioritizing health, Zambia could pave the way for a brighter future for its citizens.

Dr. Mwansa watched them go, filled with hope for the impact they would make as future leaders and advocates for health equity in Zambia. He knew that with their passion and dedication, they would continue to champion the cause of health and well-being, driving positive change in their communities and beyond.

Social Protection and Welfare Systems in Zambia

The lecture hall was abuzz with anticipation as Dr. Mwansa prepared to delve into the vital topic of social protection and welfare systems in Zambia. The students, keenly aware of the importance of safety nets for vulnerable populations, listened intently, eager to learn how these systems could make a difference in people's lives.

"Good afternoon, everyone," Dr. Mwansa greeted, his voice carrying a tone of empathy and determination. "Today, we shine a spotlight on the essential role of social protection and welfare systems in ensuring the well-being of all Zambians."

He clicked a button, and the screen illuminated with images of families receiving support, community outreach programs, and government agencies working to alleviate poverty and hardship. "Social protection encompasses a range of policies and programs aimed at reducing poverty, promoting social inclusion, and protecting individuals and families from risks and vulnerabilities," Dr. Mwansa explained. "It is a cornerstone of social development and a manifestation of a compassionate society."

The next slide displayed graphs showing social protection indicators such as coverage rates, benefit levels, and expenditure allocations across different regions of Zambia. "While progress has been made in expanding social protection coverage, gaps remain," Dr. Mwansa continued. "Many Zambians still lack access to essential social services and face risks such as unemployment, illness, and old age without adequate support."

A student raised her hand. "How can we strengthen social protection systems to reach more people in need?"

"An excellent question," Dr. Mwansa replied, bringing up a slide highlighting strategies for enhancing social protection coverage. "One approach is to expand the scope and coverage of social assistance programs, such as cash transfers, food assistance, and social pensions. These programs provide immediate relief to vulnerable populations and help reduce poverty and inequality."

He then displayed images of community-based support networks and partnerships with civil society organizations. "Community-based initiatives play a crucial role in complementing formal social protection systems," Dr. Mwansa emphasized. "By mobilizing local resources and knowledge, communities can provide support to those in need and foster social solidarity."

A student in the back row raised his hand. "How can we ensure the sustainability of social protection systems in the long term?"

"Sustainability is key," Dr. Mwansa replied, transitioning to a slide showing the importance of financing and governance mechanisms. "Investing in social protection is not just a moral imperative; it is also an investment in the future. By mobilizing domestic resources, leveraging external assistance, and strengthening governance and accountability mechanisms, we can ensure the sustainability and effectiveness of social protection systems."

He then displayed graphs showing the impact of social protection programs on poverty reduction and human development outcomes. "Moreover, social protection has multiplier effects, contributing to economic growth, social cohesion, and resilience. By investing in social protection, we invest in the well-being and dignity of all Zambians."

As the lecture concluded, Dr. Mwansa left the students with a final thought. "Social protection is a fundamental human right and a powerful tool for promoting social justice and equity. By building inclusive and resilient social protection systems, we can create a more just and compassionate Zambia for all."

The students left the hall, their hearts filled with a renewed sense of purpose and commitment to building a more inclusive society. They understood that by prioritizing social protection, Zambia could create a brighter future where no one is left behind.

Dr. Mwansa watched them go, filled with hope for the impact they would make as future leaders and advocates for social justice and welfare in Zambia. He knew that with their passion and dedication, they would continue to champion the cause of social protection, driving positive change and transforming lives across the country.

Gender Equality and Women's Empowerment in Zambia

The lecture hall buzzed with anticipation as Dr. Mwansa prepared to tackle the critical topic of gender equality and women's empowerment in Zambia. The students, acutely aware of the importance of gender equity, sat up straight in their seats, ready to absorb every word from their esteemed professor.

"Good afternoon, everyone," Dr. Mwansa greeted, his voice resonating with sincerity and determination. "Today, we turn our focus to the vital issue of gender equality and women's empowerment in Zambia."

He clicked a button, and the screen lit up with images of women leaders, activists, and entrepreneurs breaking barriers and driving change. "Gender equality is not just a moral imperative; it is also essential for achieving sustainable development and social justice," Dr. Mwansa explained. "When women and girls have equal rights and opportunities, societies thrive."

The next slide displayed graphs showing gender disparities in education, employment, and political representation across different regions of Zambia. "While progress has been made in advancing gender equality, significant gaps remain," Dr. Mwansa continued. "Women and girls continue to face discrimination, violence, and unequal access to resources and opportunities."

A student raised her hand. "How can we promote gender equality and women's empowerment in Zambia?"

"An excellent question," Dr. Mwansa replied, bringing up a slide highlighting strategies for advancing gender equality. "One approach is to enact and enforce laws that protect women's rights and promote gender equality. This includes legislation against gender-based violence, discriminatory practices, and unequal pay."

He then displayed images of women participating in leadership roles and decision-making processes. "Empowering women economically and politically is also crucial," Dr. Mwansa emphasized. "By increasing women's access to education, training, finance, and leadership positions, we can unlock their full potential and enhance their agency and autonomy."

A student in the front row raised her hand. "How can we engage men and boys as allies in the fight for gender equality?"

"Engaging men and boys is essential," Dr. Mwansa replied, transitioning to a slide showing the importance of gender-transformative approaches. "By challenging harmful gender norms and stereotypes and promoting positive masculinities, we can create more inclusive and equitable societies. Men and boys have a crucial role to play as allies, advocates, and agents of change."

He then displayed graphs showing the benefits of gender equality for economic growth and social development. "Moreover, gender equality is not just the right thing to do; it is also smart economics. Investing in women and girls yields significant returns, driving economic growth, reducing poverty, and improving health and education outcomes for all."

As the lecture concluded, Dr. Mwansa left the students with a final thought. "Gender equality is a fundamental human right and a prerequisite for achieving our full potential as individuals and as a society. By working together to dismantle barriers and create opportunities for all, we can build a more just, equitable, and prosperous Zambia."

The students left the hall, their minds buzzing with new-found insights into the transformative power of gender equality and women's empowerment. They understood that by championing gender equity, Zambia could unlock the talents and contributions of all its citizens, driving progress and prosperity for generations to come.

Dr. Mwansa watched them go, filled with hope for the impact they would make as future leaders and advocates for gender equality in Zambia. He knew that with their passion and dedication, they would continue to challenge injustice, break down barriers, and build a more inclusive and equitable world for all.

Migration and Social Change in Zambia

The lecture hall brimmed with anticipation as Dr. Mwansa embarked on the intricate exploration of migration and its social implications in Zambia. The students, perched at the edge of their seats, awaited insights into this dynamic facet of societal change.

"Good afternoon, everyone," Dr. Mwansa greeted, his voice resonating with warmth and authority. "Today, we delve into the fascinating realm of migration and its impact on social dynamics in Zambia."

With a click, the screen illuminated, revealing images of bustling city streets, rural landscapes, and diverse communities. "Migration is a fundamental aspect of human history, shaping societies and cultures across the globe," Dr. Mwansa began. "In Zambia, migration has played a significant role in shaping demographic patterns, economic landscapes, and social structures."

The next slide displayed graphs depicting migration trends, both internal and international, across different regions of Zambia. "Migration takes various forms, from rural to urban migration to international migration for work, education, or refuge," Dr. Mwansa continued. "Each form of migration brings its own set of opportunities and challenges, influencing social change in profound ways."

A student raised her hand. "How does migration contribute to social change in Zambia?"

"An excellent question," Dr. Mwansa replied, bringing up a slide highlighting the transformative effects of migration.

"Migration fosters cultural exchange, diversity, and innovation, enriching the social fabric of Zambia. It also drives urbanization, as rural migrants seek better opportunities in urban centers, leading to changes in lifestyle, values, and social norms."

He then displayed images of migrant communities and cultural celebrations. "Moreover, migration contributes to social cohesion and solidarity, as migrants form networks of support and belonging in their new environments. These networks often transcend geographic boundaries, connecting individuals and communities across regions and nations."

A student in the back row raised his hand. "What are some of the challenges associated with migration in Zambia?"

"Challenges abound," Dr. Mwansa replied, transitioning to a slide showing the complexities of migration. "For one, migration can exacerbate urbanization, leading to overcrowding, strain on infrastructure, and competition for resources. It can also contribute to social tensions, as host communities may perceive migrants as competitors for jobs and services."

He then displayed graphs showing the impact of migration on social cohesion and integration. "Moreover, migration can pose risks to migrants themselves, such as exploitation, discrimination, and social exclusion. Addressing these challenges requires comprehensive policies and programs that protect the rights of migrants, promote social inclusion, and harness the potential benefits of migration for all."

As the lecture concluded, Dr. Mwansa left the students with a final thought. "Migration is a complex and multifaceted phenomenon, shaping the dynamics of society in profound ways. By understanding its drivers, impacts, and challenges, we can navigate its waters more effectively and harness its potential for positive social change."

The students left the hall, their minds buzzing with new-found insights into the intricate interplay between migration and social dynamics. They understood that by embracing diversity, fostering inclusivity, and addressing the challenges of migration, Zambia could build a more resilient, cohesive, and vibrant society.

Dr. Mwansa watched them go, filled with hope for the impact they would make as future leaders and advocates for social justice and cohesion in Zambia. He knew that with their passion and dedication, they would continue to navigate the complexities of migration, driving positive change and building a brighter future for all.

5

Chapter 5: Political Development

Governance and Institutions in Zambia

The atmosphere in the lecture hall crackled with anticipation as Dr. Mwansa prepared to dissect the intricacies of political development, beginning with governance and institutions in Zambia. The students, eager to comprehend the mechanisms that shape their nation's political landscape, leaned forward in their seats, ready to absorb every word from their esteemed professor.

"Good afternoon, everyone," Dr. Mwansa greeted, his voice resonating with authority and gravitas. "Today, we embark on a journey to explore the foundations of political development in Zambia, starting with an examination of governance and institutions."

With a click, the screen illuminated, revealing images of government buildings, parliamentary sessions, and political leaders engaged in decision-making processes. "Governance and institutions form the backbone of any political system,"

Dr. Mwansa began. "In Zambia, they provide the framework through which power is exercised, laws are made, and public affairs are managed."

The next slide displayed diagrams depicting the structure of Zambia's government, including the executive, legislative, and judicial branches. "Zambia operates under a democratic system of governance, characterized by the separation of powers and checks and balances," Dr. Mwansa continued. "This ensures accountability, transparency, and the rule of law."

A student raised her hand. "How do governance and institutions influence political stability and effectiveness in Zambia?"

"An excellent question," Dr. Mwansa replied, bringing up a slide highlighting the role of governance in fostering political stability and effectiveness. "Strong and effective institutions are essential for ensuring political stability, promoting economic development, and safeguarding the rights and freedoms of citizens. They provide the framework for peaceful and orderly governance, enabling the resolution of conflicts and the fulfillment of public needs."

He then displayed images of government officials and civil servants carrying out their duties. "Moreover, good governance enhances the efficiency and effectiveness of public services, ensuring that resources are allocated equitably and used judiciously to meet the needs of all citizens."

A student in the front row raised his hand. "How can we strengthen governance and institutions in Zambia?"

"Strengthening governance and institutions requires a multi-faceted approach," Dr. Mwansa replied, transitioning to a slide showing strategies for reform and improvement.

"This includes promoting transparency and accountability in government operations, enhancing the capacity and professionalism of public institutions, and fostering a culture of civic engagement and participation."

He then displayed graphs showing the impact of governance reforms on political stability and economic development. "Moreover, building strong and resilient institutions is a long-term endeavor that requires sustained commitment and investment from all stakeholders. By working together to strengthen governance and institutions, we can build a more stable, prosperous, and democratic Zambia."

As the lecture concluded, Dr. Mwansa left the students with a final thought. "Governance and institutions are the cornerstones of political development. By upholding the principles of democracy, transparency, and accountability, we can build a political system that serves the interests of all Zambians and paves the way for a brighter future."

The students left the hall, their minds buzzing with new-found insights into the complexities of political development. They understood that by championing good governance and strong institutions, Zambia could build a more resilient and inclusive democracy, ensuring a better future for generations to come.

Dr. Mwansa watched them go, filled with hope for the impact they would make as future leaders and advocates for political reform in Zambia. He knew that with their passion and dedication, they would continue to strive for a more just, transparent, and democratic society, driving positive change and progress for all.

Democracy and Political Participation in Zambia

The lecture hall was filled with eager anticipation as Dr. Mwansa continued his exploration of political development in Zambia, shifting the focus to democracy and political participation. The students, keenly aware of their role as future citizens and leaders, listened intently, ready to delve into the intricacies of democratic governance.

"Good afternoon, everyone," Dr. Mwansa greeted, his voice carrying a tone of reverence and enthusiasm. "Today, we delve deeper into the heart of Zambia's political landscape, examining the principles of democracy and the importance of political participation."

With a click, the screen illuminated, revealing images of voting booths, election rallies, and citizens engaging in civic activities. "Democracy lies at the core of Zambia's political system, providing the framework for citizen participation, accountability, and the peaceful transfer of power," Dr. Mwansa began. "It is a system built on the principles of equality, freedom, and respect for human rights."

The next slide displayed graphs showing voter turnout rates, political party affiliations, and levels of civic engagement across different regions of Zambia. "Political participation is the lifeblood of democracy," Dr. Mwansa continued. "It empowers citizens to voice their concerns, shape public policies, and hold their leaders accountable."

A student raised her hand. "How can we ensure that political participation is inclusive and equitable for all Zambians?"

"An excellent question," Dr. Mwansa replied, bringing up a slide highlighting strategies for promoting inclusive political participation. "One approach is to remove barriers to participation, such as voter registration requirements, language barriers, and discrimination. This includes providing voter education and outreach programs to ensure that all citizens have the information and resources they need to participate effectively."

He then displayed images of civic education initiatives and voter registration drives. "Moreover, fostering a culture of political tolerance and dialogue is essential," Dr. Mwansa emphasized. "By promoting respect for diverse perspectives and encouraging constructive debate, we can create an environment where all voices are heard and valued."

A student in the back row raised his hand. "How can we encourage youth participation in politics and governance?"

"Youth participation is vital for the vitality of democracy," Dr. Mwansa replied, transitioning to a slide showing the importance of youth engagement. "By providing opportunities for youth to engage in decision-making processes, such as youth councils, advisory boards, and community projects, we can harness their energy, creativity, and idealism to drive positive change."

He then displayed graphs showing the impact of youth participation on democratic governance. "Moreover, investing in civic education and leadership development programs for youth can help build the next generation of informed and active citizens, ensuring a vibrant and inclusive democracy for years to come."

As the lecture concluded, Dr. Mwansa left the students with a final thought. "Democracy is not a spectator sport; it requires active engagement and participation from all citizens. By embracing the principles of democracy and fostering a culture of political participation, we can build a more inclusive, responsive, and resilient Zambia."

The students left the hall, their minds buzzing with new-found insights into the power of democracy and political participation. They understood that by engaging actively in the political process, they could shape the future of their country and contribute to a more just and prosperous society.

Dr. Mwansa watched them go, filled with hope for the impact they would make as future leaders and advocates for democracy in Zambia. He knew that with their passion and dedication, they would continue to uphold the principles of democracy, driving positive change and progress for all.

Corruption and Accountability: Zambian Challenges

The lecture hall fell into a hushed silence as Dr. Mwansa broached the sensitive topic of corruption and accountability in Zambia. The students, their expressions solemn, braced themselves for a candid exploration of one of the nation's most pressing challenges.

"Good afternoon, everyone," Dr. Mwansa began, his voice tinged with gravity and resolve. "Today, we confront a harsh reality: the pervasive issue of corruption and the imperative of accountability in Zambia's political landscape."

With a click, the screen illuminated, revealing images of bribery, embezzlement, and the erosion of public trust. "Corruption is a cancer that eats away at the fabric of society," Dr. Mwansa stated solemnly. "It undermines the rule of law, distorts economic opportunities, and erodes public trust in government institutions."

The next slide displayed graphs showing corruption perception indices and instances of graft across different sectors of Zambian society. "Despite efforts to combat corruption, challenges persist," Dr. Mwansa continued. "Weak enforcement mechanisms, lack of transparency, and impunity for perpetrators have allowed corruption to flourish, undermining development and eroding public confidence in the government."

A student raised her hand. "How can we tackle corruption and promote accountability in Zambia?"

"An excellent question," Dr. Mwansa replied, bringing up a slide highlighting strategies for combating corruption and enhancing accountability. "One approach is to strengthen anti-corruption institutions and mechanisms, such as law enforcement agencies, anti-corruption commissions, and oversight bodies. These institutions play a crucial role in investigating and prosecuting cases of corruption, holding perpetrators accountable, and recovering stolen assets."

He then displayed images of whistle-blowers and civil society activists advocating for transparency and accountability. "Moreover, promoting transparency and public participation can help prevent corruption and foster accountability," Dr. Mwansa emphasized. "By ensuring open access to information, engaging citizens in decision-making processes, and promoting a culture of integrity and ethics, we can create an environment where corruption is less likely to thrive."

A student in the front row raised his hand. "How can we build a culture of accountability in Zambia?"

"Building a culture of accountability requires leadership and commitment at all levels of society," Dr. Mwansa replied, transitioning to a slide showing the importance of leadership and civic engagement. "Leaders must lead by example, demonstrating integrity, honesty, and commitment to the public good. Citizens, on the other hand, must hold their leaders accountable, demanding transparency, accountability, and responsiveness in governance."

He then displayed graphs showing the impact of account-ability mechanisms on reducing corruption and promoting development. "Moreover, fostering a culture of accountability requires building strong institutions, promoting the rule of law, and ensuring equal access to justice for all," Dr. Mwansa concluded. "By working together to tackle corruption and promote accountability, we can build a more just, transparent, and prosperous Zambia for all."

As the lecture concluded, Dr. Mwansa left the students with a final thought. "Corruption and accountability are not just issues of governance; they are moral imperatives. By confronting corruption head-on and promoting a culture of accountability, we can build a brighter future for Zambia, where integrity, justice, and trust in government prevail."

The students left the hall, their minds swirling with the weight of the challenges ahead. They understood that by confronting corruption and demanding accountability, they could help pave the way for a more just and equitable society.

Dr. Mwansa watched them go, filled with hope for the impact they would make as future leaders and advocates for integrity in Zambia. He knew that with their passion and dedication, they would continue to fight against corruption, driving positive change and progress for all.

Conflict and Peacebuilding in Zambia

The lecture hall brimmed with anticipation as Dr. Mwansa embarked on a poignant discussion about conflict and peacebuilding in Zambia. The students, their faces reflecting a mixture of curiosity and concern, awaited insights into the delicate balance between stability and discord in their nation.

"Good afternoon, everyone," Dr. Mwansa greeted, his voice resonating with empathy and determination. "Today, we confront the sobering reality of conflict and the imperative of peacebuilding in Zambia."

With a click, the screen illuminated, revealing images of protests, unrest, and community reconciliation efforts. "Conflict, whether internal or external, poses a significant threat to the fabric of society," Dr. Mwansa began solemnly. "It disrupts lives, undermines social cohesion, and hampers progress and development."

The next slide displayed graphs showing conflict hotspots and instances of violence across different regions of Zambia. "While Zambia has been fortunate to avoid large-scale conflicts, localized tensions and grievances persist," Dr. Mwansa continued. "These conflicts may stem from various factors, including ethnic tensions, land disputes, political rivalries, and socioeconomic inequalities."

A student raised her hand. "How can we address conflicts and promote peacebuilding in Zambia?"

"An excellent question," Dr. Mwansa replied, bringing up a slide highlighting strategies for conflict resolution and peacebuilding. "One approach is to address the root causes of conflict through dialogue, mediation, and reconciliation. This involves creating spaces for dialogue and negotiation, facilitating peaceful resolution of disputes, and promoting understanding and empathy among conflicting parties."

He then displayed images of peace conferences and community reconciliation ceremonies. "Moreover, building resilient and inclusive institutions is essential for preventing conflicts and sustaining peace," Dr. Mwansa emphasized. "By promoting good governance, equitable access to resources, and social justice, we can address the underlying grievances that fuel conflicts and build a more stable and peaceful society."

A student in the back row raised his hand. "How can we engage youth and marginalized groups in peace-building efforts?"

"Youth and marginalized groups have a crucial role to play in peace-building," Dr. Mwansa replied, transitioning to a slide showing the importance of youth and community engagement. "By providing opportunities for meaningful participation in decision-making processes, promoting youth-led initiatives, and addressing the specific needs and concerns of marginalized communities, we can empower them to become agents of positive change and peace."

He then displayed graphs showing the impact of youth and community engagement on conflict prevention and peace-building. "Moreover, investing in education, skills training, and economic opportunities for youth can help address the root causes of conflict and build resilience against violence," Dr. Mwansa concluded. "By working together to address conflicts and promote peace-building, we can build a more resilient, cohesive, and peaceful Zambia for all."

As the lecture concluded, Dr. Mwansa left the students with a final thought. "Conflict may be inevitable, but peace is achievable. By fostering understanding, dialogue, and cooperation, we can build a future where peace prevails, and all Zambians can thrive."

The students left the hall, their hearts heavy with the weight of the challenges ahead. They understood that by embracing peace-building efforts, they could help pave the way for a more harmonious and prosperous society.

Dr. Mwansa watched them go, filled with hope for the impact they would make as future leaders and advocates for peace in Zambia. He knew that with their passion and dedication, they would continue to work tirelessly to build a more peaceful and inclusive Zambia for generations to come.

Policy Making and Implementation in Zambia

The lecture hall buzzed with anticipation as Dr. Mwansa delved into the intricate workings of policy making and implementation in Zambia. The students, keenly aware of the pivotal role policies play in shaping their nation's future, leaned forward in their seats, eager to grasp the complexities of governance.

"Good afternoon, everyone," Dr. Mwansa greeted, his voice resonating with authority and conviction. "Today, we explore the critical process of policy making and implementation in Zambia."

With a click, the screen illuminated, revealing images of lawmakers, policymakers, and stakeholders engaged in discussions and debates. "Policy making is the foundation of governance, guiding decision-making processes and shaping the direction of the nation," Dr. Mwansa began. "In Zambia, policies are formulated to address a wide range of issues, from economic development to social welfare, and from environmental conservation to political reform."

The next slide displayed diagrams depicting the policy making cycle, from agenda setting to evaluation and feedback. "Policy making is a complex and iterative process," Dr. Mwansa continued. "It involves multiple stakeholders, including government agencies, civil society organizations, private sector actors, and the public, working together to identify problems, develop solutions, and implement interventions."

A student raised her hand. "How are policies formulated and enacted in Zambia?"

"An excellent question," Dr. Mwansa replied, bringing up a slide highlighting the stages of the policy making process. "Policy formulation typically begins with agenda setting, where issues are identified and prioritized based on their urgency and importance. This is followed by policy analysis, where various options are evaluated, and decisions are made based on evidence and expert opinion."

He then displayed images of policymakers drafting legislation and consulting with stakeholders. "Once a policy is formulated, it must be translated into actionable plans and programs," Dr. Mwansa explained. "This requires coordination among government agencies, allocation of resources, and engagement with relevant stakeholders to ensure effective implementation."

A student in the front row raised his hand. "What are some of the challenges in policy implementation in Zambia?"

"Policy implementation is often fraught with challenges," Dr. Mwansa replied, transitioning to a slide showing common obstacles and barriers. "These may include limited financial resources, capacity constraints, bureaucratic red tape, and resistance to change. Moreover, monitoring and evaluation mechanisms are essential for tracking progress, identifying gaps, and making adjustments as needed."

He then displayed graphs showing the impact of effective policy implementation on development outcomes. "However, despite these challenges, successful policy implementation is achievable with strong leadership, effective coordination, and active engagement with stakeholders," Dr. Mwansa concluded. "By working together to overcome obstacles and address implementation gaps, we can ensure that policies translate into tangible benefits for all Zambians."

As the lecture concluded, Dr. Mwansa left the students with a final thought. "Policy making and implementation are not just bureaucratic processes; they are the means by which we translate our aspirations into action. By embracing evidence-based decision-making, fostering collaboration, and prioritizing accountability, we can build a more responsive, inclusive, and effective governance system in Zambia."

The students left the hall, their minds buzzing with new-found insights into the complexities of policy making and implementation. They understood that by engaging actively in the policy process, they could help shape the future of their country and contribute to a more just and prosperous society.

Dr. Mwansa watched them go, filled with hope for the impact they would make as future leaders and policymakers in Zambia. He knew that with their passion and dedication, they would continue to strive for effective governance, driving positive change and progress for all.

Role of Civil Society in Zambia's Development

The lecture hall hummed with anticipation as Dr. Mwansa delved into the vital role of civil society in Zambia's development. The students, recognizing the significance of grassroots movements and advocacy, leaned forward in their seats, eager to understand how ordinary citizens could drive change.

"Good afternoon, everyone," Dr. Mwansa greeted, his voice imbued with admiration for the power of collective action. "Today, we shine a spotlight on the unsung heroes of Zambia's development: civil society organizations."

With a click, the screen illuminated, revealing images of community organizers, activists, and volunteers rallying for various causes. "Civil society plays a crucial role in amplifying the voices of the marginalized, holding the government accountable, and driving social change," Dr. Mwansa began. "In Zambia, civil society organizations encompass a diverse range of groups, including NGOs, grassroots movements, advocacy networks, and community-based organizations."

The next slide displayed diagrams depicting the interconnected web of civil society actors and their areas of focus. "Civil society serves as a bridge between citizens and the government, advocating for policies and programs that address pressing social issues," Dr. Mwansa continued. "They provide essential services, promote human rights, and empower communities to take charge of their own development."

A student raised her hand. "How do civil society organizations influence policy and decision-making in Zambia?"

"An excellent question," Dr. Mwansa replied, bringing up a slide highlighting the mechanisms through which civil society organizations exert influence. "Civil society organizations engage in various activities, including advocacy, research, and public education, to shape public discourse and influence policy decisions. They participate in policy forums, submit policy briefs, and mobilize public support to push for reforms and changes."

He then displayed images of civil society activists lobbying policymakers and organizing protests. "Moreover, civil society organizations serve as watchdogs, monitoring government actions, exposing corruption, and holding leaders accountable for their decisions," Dr. Mwansa emphasized. "By providing independent oversight and promoting transparency, they help ensure that government policies and programs are responsive to the needs of the people."

A student in the back row raised his hand. "How can we strengthen civil society in Zambia?"

"Strengthening civil society requires a supportive environment that respects and protects the rights of citizens to organize, assemble, and express their views," Dr. Mwansa replied, transitioning to a slide showing strategies for supporting civil society. "This includes enacting laws and policies that facilitate the operation of civil society organizations, providing funding and technical assistance to build their capacity, and fostering collaboration and networking among different groups."

He then displayed graphs showing the impact of civil society engagement on development outcomes. "Moreover, promoting a culture of civic engagement and participation is essential for nurturing an active and vibrant civil society," Dr. Mwansa concluded. "By working together to strengthen civil society, we can build a more inclusive, democratic, and resilient Zambia for all."

As the lecture concluded, Dr. Mwansa left the students with a final thought. "Civil society is the heartbeat of democracy, the driving force behind social progress, and the guardian of human rights. By empowering civil society organizations and supporting their efforts, we can build a more just, equitable, and prosperous Zambia for generations to come."

The students left the hall, their minds ablaze with newfound appreciation for the transformative power of civil society. They understood that by actively engaging with civil society organizations, they could become catalysts for change and champions for a better Zambia.

Dr. Mwansa watched them go, filled with hope for the impact they would make as future leaders and advocates for social justice and democracy in Zambia. He knew that with their passion and dedication, they would continue to work tirelessly to build a more inclusive and equitable society for all.

6

Chapter 6: Environmental Sustainability

Climate Change and its Impacts on Zambia

The lecture hall was charged with a sense of urgency as Dr. Mwansa began to unravel the intricate challenges of environmental sustainability, focusing on the looming specter of climate change and its profound impacts on Zambia. The students, their faces etched with concern, awaited insights into the existential threat facing their nation.

"Good afternoon, everyone," Dr. Mwansa greeted, his voice echoing with a solemn tone. "Today, we confront one of the most pressing issues of our time: climate change and its far-reaching consequences on Zambia's environment and society."

With a click, the screen illuminated, revealing images of melting glaciers, rising sea levels, and extreme weather events. "Climate change poses an existential threat to our planet, disrupting ecosystems, exacerbating natural disasters, and threatening the lives and livelihoods of millions," Dr. Mwansa began. "In Zambia, the impacts of climate change are already being felt, from erratic rainfall patterns to prolonged droughts and increased frequency of extreme weather events."

The next slide displayed graphs showing temperature trends, precipitation patterns, and the alarming rate of deforestation in Zambia. "Climate change is not just an environmental issue; it is a development challenge that requires urgent action," Dr. Mwansa continued. "It threatens food security, water resources, and public health, exacerbating existing vulnerabilities and deepening inequalities."

A student raised her hand. "How can we mitigate the impacts of climate change in Zambia?"

"An excellent question," Dr. Mwansa replied, bringing up a slide highlighting strategies for climate change mitigation and adaptation. "Mitigating the impacts of climate change requires a multi-faceted approach, including reducing greenhouse gas emissions, enhancing resilience to climate-related hazards, and promoting sustainable development practices."

He then displayed images of renewable energy projects, reforestation initiatives, and climate-resilient infrastructure. "Moreover, investing in renewable energy, such as solar and wind power, can help reduce our reliance on fossil fuels and lower our carbon footprint," Dr. Mwansa explained. "By promoting sustainable land management practices, protecting biodiversity, and strengthening early warning systems, we can build resilience to climate change and minimize its impacts on vulnerable communities."

A student in the front row raised his hand. "How can individuals contribute to climate action in Zambia?"

"Individual actions play a crucial role in addressing climate change," Dr. Mwansa replied, transitioning to a slide showing everyday actions to reduce carbon emissions and promote sustainability. "This includes conserving energy, reducing waste, using public transportation, and supporting sustainable businesses and products."

He then displayed graphs showing the collective impact of individual actions on mitigating climate change. "Moreover, raising awareness and advocating for climate action can help mobilize public support and galvanize political will," Dr. Mwansa concluded. "By working together at all levels of society, we can confront the challenge of climate change and build a more sustainable and resilient Zambia for future generations."

As the lecture concluded, Dr. Mwansa left the students with a final thought. "Climate change is the defining issue of our time, but it is also an opportunity for positive change. By embracing sustainable practices, fostering innovation, and working together to address climate change, we can build a future where people and planet thrive in harmony."

The students left the hall, their minds buzzing with new-found determination to confront the challenge of climate change head-on. They understood that by taking action now, they could help safeguard the future of their country and the world.

Dr. Mwansa watched them go, filled with hope for the impact they would make as future leaders and stewards of the environment in Zambia. He knew that with their passion and dedication, they would continue to champion climate action and drive positive change for the benefit of all.

Natural Resource Management in Zambia

The atmosphere in the lecture hall shifted as Dr. Mwansa delved into the intricate topic of natural resource management in Zambia. The students, their faces reflecting a mixture of curiosity and concern, leaned forward in their seats, eager to understand how their nation's rich natural resources could be preserved and utilized sustainably.

"Good afternoon, everyone," Dr. Mwansa greeted, his voice resonating with authority and passion. "Today, we explore the vital importance of natural resource management in Zambia's sustainable development."

With a click, the screen illuminated, revealing images of lush forests, expansive savannas, and sparkling rivers. "Zambia is blessed with abundant natural resources, including minerals, forests, water, and biodiversity," Dr. Mwansa began. "These resources are not only essential for supporting livelihoods and economic growth but also for maintaining ecosystem health and resilience."

The next slide displayed graphs showing the distribution of natural resources across different regions of Zambia. "However, the sustainable management of these resources poses significant challenges," Dr. Mwansa continued. "From deforestation and habitat loss to water pollution and over-extraction of minerals, human activities are placing immense pressure on our natural ecosystems."

A student raised her hand. "How can we ensure the sustainable management of Zambia's natural resources?"

"An excellent question," Dr. Mwansa replied, bringing up a slide highlighting strategies for sustainable natural resource management. "Sustainable resource management requires a holistic approach that balances economic development with environmental conservation and social equity."

He then displayed images of protected areas, community-based conservation initiatives, and sustainable forestry practices. "One approach is to promote community-based natural resource management, empowering local communities to manage and benefit from their natural resources sustainably," Dr. Mwansa explained. "By providing incentives for conservation, supporting traditional knowledge and practices, and fostering collaboration between communities and government agencies, we can protect biodiversity and ecosystems while promoting local development."

A student in the back row raised his hand. "How can we address illegal logging, mining, and poaching in Zambia?"

"Addressing illegal activities requires a coordinated effort involving law enforcement, community engagement, and international cooperation," Dr. Mwansa replied, transitioning to a slide showing strategies for combating illegal resource extraction and wildlife crime. "This includes strengthening enforcement mechanisms, enhancing surveillance and monitoring systems, and raising awareness about the impacts of illegal activities on ecosystems and communities."

He then displayed graphs showing the decline in illegal activities following effective enforcement measures. "Moreover, promoting alternative livelihoods and economic opportunities for communities dependent on natural resources can help reduce their reliance on illegal activities," Dr. Mwansa concluded. "By working together to address the root causes of illegal resource extraction and wildlife crime, we can protect our natural heritage and ensure a sustainable future for Zambia."

As the lecture concluded, Dr. Mwansa left the students with a final thought. "Natural resources are the foundation of our prosperity, but they are also a finite and vulnerable asset. By embracing sustainable resource management practices, we can preserve our natural heritage for future generations and build a more resilient and equitable Zambia."

The students left the hall, their minds buzzing with new-found insights into the importance of natural resource man-agement. They understood that by adopting sustainable practices, they could help safeguard Zambia's natural wealth and contribute to a more sustainable and prosperous future.

Dr. Mwansa watched them go, filled with hope for the impact they would make as future stewards of Zambia's natural heritage. He knew that with their passion and dedication, they would continue to champion sustainable resource management and drive positive change for the benefit of all.

Sustainable Agriculture and Food Security in Zambia

The lecture hall brimmed with anticipation as Dr. Mwansa embarked on a poignant discussion about sustainable agricul-ture and food security in Zambia. The students, recognizing the pivotal role of agriculture in their nation's development, leaned forward in their seats, eager to understand how to ensure food security while protecting the environment.

"Good afternoon, everyone," Dr. Mwansa greeted, his voice tinged with gravitas and determination. "Today, we explore the critical nexus between sustainable agriculture and food security in Zambia."

With a click, the screen illuminated, revealing images of

verdant fields, bustling markets, and farmers tending to their crops. "Agriculture is the backbone of Zambia's economy, providing livelihoods for the majority of our population and ensuring food security for our nation," Dr. Mwansa began. "However, traditional farming practices and environmental degradation threaten the long-term viability of our agricultural systems."

The next slide displayed graphs showing the challenges of soil erosion, water scarcity, and declining crop yields in Zambia. "Sustainable agriculture offers a pathway to address these challenges, ensuring that we can meet the nutritional needs of our growing population while safeguarding the health of our environment," Dr. Mwansa continued. "It involves adopting practices that promote soil health, conserve water, and protect biodiversity, while also enhancing the resilience of farming communities to climate change."

A student raised her hand. "How can we promote sustainable agriculture in Zambia?"

"An excellent question," Dr. Mwansa replied, bringing up a slide highlighting strategies for promoting sustainable agriculture. "Promoting sustainable agriculture requires a multifaceted approach that addresses the needs of smallholder farmers, promotes innovation and technology adoption, and fosters collaboration between government, civil society, and the private sector."

He then displayed images of conservation agriculture, agroforestry, and precision farming techniques. "One approach is to promote conservation agriculture practices, such as minimum tillage, crop rotation, and mulching, which help improve soil health, conserve water, and reduce greenhouse gas emissions," Dr. Mwansa explained. "By providing training, technical support, and access to inputs, we can empower farmers to adopt sustainable practices and improve their livelihoods."

A student in the front row raised his hand. "How can we ensure food security in the face of climate change and other challenges?"

"Ensuring food security requires a holistic approach that addresses both supply and demand-side factors," Dr. Mwansa replied, transitioning to a slide showing strategies for enhancing food security. "This includes investing in agricultural research and development, improving access to markets and finance for smallholder farmers, and strengthening social safety nets to protect vulnerable populations during times of crisis."

He then displayed graphs showing the impact of sustainable agriculture on food security indicators. "Moreover, promoting diversified and resilient food systems, supporting small-scale food producers, and reducing food waste can help ensure that nutritious and affordable food is available for all Zambians," Dr. Mwansa concluded. "By working together to promote sustainable agriculture and enhance food security, we can build a more resilient and equitable Zambia for future generations."

As the lecture concluded, Dr. Mwansa left the students with a final thought. "Sustainable agriculture is not just about feeding our nation; it is about ensuring the long-term health and prosperity of our people and our planet. By embracing sustainable practices and investing in the future of agriculture, we can build a more food-secure and resilient Zambia for all."

The students left the hall, their minds buzzing with new-found insights into the importance of sustainable agriculture and food security. They understood that by promoting sustainable farming practices, they could help ensure a brighter future for Zambia and its people.

Dr. Mwansa watched them go, filled with hope for the impact they would make as future leaders and innovators in agriculture. He knew that with their passion and dedication, they would continue to champion sustainable agriculture and drive positive change for the benefit of all.

Renewable Energy and Green Technologies in Zambia

The lecture hall crackled with energy as Dr. Mwansa delved into the transformative potential of renewable energy and green technologies in Zambia. The students, their faces illuminated with curiosity and excitement, leaned forward in their seats, eager to explore how innovation could drive sustainable development in their country.

"Good afternoon, everyone," Dr. Mwansa greeted, his voice vibrant with enthusiasm and optimism. "Today, we embark on a journey into the world of renewable energy and green technologies, and their profound impact on Zambia's sustainable future."

With a click, the screen illuminated, revealing images of wind turbines, solar panels, and hydroelectric dams. "Renewable energy holds the key to powering our nation while reducing our reliance on fossil fuels and mitigating the impacts of climate change," Dr. Mwansa began. "In Zambia, we are blessed with abundant renewable energy resources, including solar, wind, hydro, and biomass."

The next slide displayed graphs showing the potential of renewable energy sources to meet Zambia's growing energy demand. "Renewable energy not only offers a cleaner and more sustainable alternative to fossil fuels but also presents an opportunity for economic growth and job creation," Dr. Mwansa continued. "By harnessing our renewable energy potential, we can stimulate investment, promote innovation, and build a more resilient energy infrastructure for our nation."

A student raised her hand. "How can we accelerate the adoption of renewable energy in Zambia?"

"An excellent question," Dr. Mwansa replied, bringing up a slide highlighting strategies for promoting renewable energy adoption. "Accelerating the adoption of renewable energy requires a supportive policy and regulatory framework, incentives for investment, and public awareness and education campaigns."

He then displayed images of solar installations, wind farms, and mini-grid systems. "One approach is to promote decentralized and off-grid renewable energy solutions, particularly in rural and remote areas where access to electricity is limited," Dr. Mwansa explained. "By providing incentives for investment in renewable energy projects, streamlining permitting processes, and offering financing options, we can encourage private sector participation and unlock the full potential of renewable energy in Zambia."

A student in the front row raised his hand. "What role can green technologies play in promoting sustainable development in Zambia?"

"Green technologies offer innovative solutions for addressing environmental challenges and promoting sustainable development across various sectors," Dr. Mwansa replied, transitioning to a slide showing examples of green technologies.

"From energy-efficient appliances and smart grids to electric vehicles and green building materials, green technologies can help reduce resource consumption, minimize waste, and mitigate pollution."

He then displayed graphs showing the potential environmental and economic benefits of green technologies. "Moreover, promoting research and development in green technologies, fostering partnerships between academia, industry, and government, and providing support for technology transfer and capacity building can help accelerate their adoption and deployment," Dr. Mwansa concluded. "By embracing renewable energy and green technologies, we can build a more sustainable and prosperous Zambia for future generations."

As the lecture concluded, Dr. Mwansa left the students with a final thought. "Renewable energy and green technologies are not just about powering our homes and businesses; they are about powering our future. By investing in innovation and sustainability, we can build a more resilient, equitable, and prosperous Zambia for all."

The students left the hall, their minds buzzing with newfound excitement and inspiration. They understood that by embracing renewable energy and green technologies, they could help shape a brighter and more sustainable future for Zambia and its people.

Dr. Mwansa watched them go, filled with hope for the impact they would make as future leaders and innovators in renewable energy and green technology. He knew that with their passion and dedication, they would continue to drive positive change and build a more sustainable world for all.

Environmental Policies and Legislation in Zambia

The lecture hall was steeped in anticipation as Dr. Mwansa delved into the intricate world of environmental policies and legislation in Zambia. The students, their faces alight with curiosity and determination, leaned forward in their seats, eager to understand how laws and regulations could safeguard their country's natural heritage.

"Good afternoon, everyone," Dr. Mwansa greeted, his voice echoing with authority and conviction. "Today, we explore the cornerstone of environmental governance: policies and legislation designed to protect and preserve Zambia's rich natural heritage."

With a click, the screen illuminated, revealing images of lush forests, majestic wildlife, and pristine rivers. "Zambia boasts a wealth of natural resources, from the vast wilderness of its national parks to the fertile soils of its farmland," Dr. Mwansa began. "However, the sustainable management and conservation of these resources require a robust legal framework that balances economic development with environmental protection."

The next slide displayed diagrams depicting the hierarchy of environmental laws and regulations in Zambia. "Environmental policies and legislation in Zambia span a wide range of sectors, including forestry, wildlife, water, mining, and land use planning," Dr. Mwansa continued. "These laws establish standards, guidelines, and mechanisms for regulating human activities, preventing pollution, and conserving biodiversity."

A student raised her hand. "How do environmental policies and legislation impact sustainable development in Zambia?"

"An excellent question," Dr. Mwansa replied, bringing up

a slide highlighting the role of environmental policies in promoting sustainable development. "Environmental policies provide the legal and regulatory framework for integrating environmental considerations into development planning, decision-making, and implementation."

He then displayed images of environmental impact assessments, protected area management plans, and pollution control measures. "By requiring developers to assess and mitigate the environmental impacts of their projects, enforcing pollution control standards, and promoting sustainable land use practices, environmental policies help minimize negative externalities and ensure that development is carried out in a sustainable manner," Dr. Mwansa explained.

A student in the back row raised his hand. "How can we strengthen environmental governance in Zambia?"

"Strengthening environmental governance requires a multi-pronged approach that involves improving legal enforcement, enhancing institutional capacity, and promoting public participation," Dr. Mwansa replied, transitioning to a slide showing strategies for enhancing environmental governance. "This includes strengthening the capacity of regulatory agencies, providing training and technical assistance to enforcement personnel, and raising awareness about environmental rights and responsibilities among the public."

He then displayed graphs showing the correlation between effective environmental governance and sustainable development outcomes. "Moreover, promoting transparency, accountability, and stakeholder engagement in decision-making processes can help build trust and legitimacy in environmental governance," Dr. Mwansa concluded. "By working together to strengthen our environmental laws and institutions, we can ensure the sustainable management and conservation of Zambia's natural heritage for future generations."

As the lecture concluded, Dr. Mwansa left the students with a final thought. "Environmental policies and legislation are not just legal instruments; they are tools for building a more sustainable and resilient Zambia. By embracing environmental governance and upholding our environmental laws, we can safeguard our natural heritage and ensure a brighter future for all."

The students left the hall, their minds buzzing with new-found insights into the importance of environmental governance. They understood that by advocating for stronger environmental laws and regulations, they could help protect Zambia's natural heritage and promote sustainable development.

Dr. Mwansa watched them go, filled with hope for the impact they would make as future stewards of Zambia's environment. He knew that with their passion and dedication, they would continue to champion environmental protection and drive positive change for the benefit of all.

Community-Based Conservation in Zambia

The lecture hall buzzed with anticipation as Dr. Mwansa delved into the captivating world of community-based conservation in Zambia. The students, their faces radiant with curiosity and eagerness, leaned forward in their seats, ready to embark on a journey into the heart of grassroots conservation efforts.

"Good afternoon, everyone," Dr. Mwansa greeted, his voice resonating with warmth and passion. "Today, we shine a spotlight on the power of community-based conservation and its pivotal role in safeguarding Zambia's natural heritage."

With a click, the screen illuminated, revealing images of vibrant communities, pristine landscapes, and diverse wildlife. "Community-based conservation empowers local communities to take ownership of their natural resources and participate in their sustainable management and conservation," Dr. Mwansa began. "In Zambia, where the majority of our population resides in rural areas, community-based conservation offers a holistic approach to conservation that integrates social, economic, and environmental considerations."

The next slide displayed diagrams depicting the principles of community-based conservation and its benefits for both people and nature. "Community-based conservation fosters a sense of stewardship and responsibility among local communities, empowering them to protect and manage their natural resources sustainably," Dr. Mwansa continued. "By engaging communities as partners in conservation, we can achieve better conservation outcomes, improve livelihoods, and promote social cohesion and resilience."

A student raised her hand. "How do community-based conservation initiatives operate in Zambia?"

"An excellent question," Dr. Mwansa replied, bringing up a slide highlighting examples of community-based conservation initiatives in Zambia. "Community-based conservation initiatives in Zambia take various forms, from community-owned wildlife conservancies and eco-tourism ventures to sustainable natural resource management projects and community-based forest management."

He then displayed images of community-led patrols, conservation workshops, and eco-friendly enterprises. "These initiatives are driven by local knowledge, traditions, and priorities, and are tailored to the needs and aspirations of each community," Dr. Mwansa explained. "By providing training, technical support, and access to resources, we can empower communities to develop and implement their conservation strategies."

A student in the front row raised his hand. "How can we support and scale up community-based conservation efforts in Zambia?"

"Supporting and scaling up community-based conservation efforts requires collaboration and partnership between government, civil society, and local communities," Dr. Mwansa replied, transitioning to a slide showing strategies for supporting community-based conservation. "This includes providing financial and technical support, promoting policy and legal reforms that recognize and support community rights and tenure, and fostering collaboration and knowledge exchange among different stakeholders."

He then displayed graphs showing the positive impact of community-based conservation on biodiversity conservation, poverty alleviation, and sustainable development. "Moreover, promoting community-based conservation can help empower marginalized groups, such as women and indigenous peoples, and promote social equity and inclusion," Dr. Mwansa concluded. "By working together to support community-based conservation, we can build a more sustainable and resilient Zambia for future generations."

As the lecture concluded, Dr. Mwansa left the students with a final thought. "Community-based conservation is not just about protecting nature; it is about empowering communities, promoting social justice, and building a more sustainable future for all. By embracing community-based conservation, we can harness the collective wisdom and ingenuity of our people to safeguard Zambia's natural heritage for generations to come."

The students left the hall, their hearts filled with inspiration and determination. They understood that by supporting community-based conservation efforts, they could play a vital role in protecting Zambia's biodiversity and promoting sustainable development.

Dr. Mwansa watched them go, filled with hope for the impact they would make as future champions of community-based conservation. He knew that with their passion and dedication, they would continue to work tirelessly to protect Zambia's natural heritage and build a brighter future for all.

7

Chapter 7: Cultural Dimensions of Development

Role of Culture in Zambia's Development

The lecture hall exuded a sense of reverence as Dr. Mwansa embarked on a captivating exploration of the cultural dimensions of development in Zambia. The students, their eyes alight with curiosity and respect, leaned forward in their seats, eager to uncover the profound influence of culture on their nation's development journey.

"Good afternoon, everyone," Dr. Mwansa greeted, his voice resonating with reverence and admiration. "Today, we embark on a journey into the heart and soul of Zambia's development: its rich and diverse cultural heritage."

With a click, the screen illuminated, revealing images of traditional ceremonies, vibrant dances, and intricate crafts. "Culture is the bedrock of Zambia's identity, shaping our beliefs, values, and traditions," Dr. Mwansa began. "It is woven into the fabric of our society, informing our ways of life, social interactions, and collective aspirations."

The next slide displayed diagrams depicting the multi-faceted role of culture in development and its profound impact on various aspects of society. "Culture plays a pivotal role in fostering social cohesion, preserving indigenous knowledge, and promoting creativity and innovation," Dr. Mwansa continued. "It serves as a source of resilience and strength, providing communities with a sense of belonging and identity in the face of change and adversity."

A student raised her hand. "How does culture contribute to economic development in Zambia?"

"An excellent question," Dr. Mwansa replied, bringing up a slide highlighting the economic significance of culture in Zambia. "Culture contributes to economic development in Zambia in various ways, from promoting tourism and cultural industries to supporting small-scale enterprises and artisanal craftsmanship."

He then displayed images of cultural festivals, heritage sites, and artisan workshops. "Cultural tourism, for example, attracts visitors from around the world, generating revenue, creating jobs, and preserving cultural heritage," Dr. Mwansa explained. "Likewise, the promotion of traditional crafts and cultural products not only provides income for artisans but also contributes to the preservation of traditional knowledge and skills."

A student in the front row raised his hand. "How can we leverage culture to promote sustainable development in Zambia?"

"Leveraging culture for sustainable development requires recognizing and respecting the diversity of cultural expressions and promoting inclusive and participatory approaches,"

Dr. Mwansa replied, transitioning to a slide showing strategies for integrating culture into development planning. "This includes supporting cultural heritage conservation, promoting intercultural dialogue and exchange, and empowering communities to participate in decision-making processes."

He then displayed graphs showing the positive impact of cultural heritage conservation on community well-being and economic development. "Moreover, promoting cultural diversity and inclusion can help build social cohesion, foster mutual understanding, and strengthen the resilience of communities in the face of social, economic, and environmental challenges," Dr. Mwansa concluded. "By embracing culture as a driver of development, we can build a more vibrant, inclusive, and sustainable Zambia for future generations."

As the lecture concluded, Dr. Mwansa left the students with a final thought. "Culture is not just a reflection of who we are; it is a powerful force for change and transformation. By honoring and preserving our cultural heritage, we can build a future that is rooted in respect, diversity, and unity."

The students left the hall, their hearts filled with a newfound appreciation for the role of culture in development. They understood that by embracing and celebrating their cultural heritage, they could contribute to a more vibrant and resilient Zambia.

Dr. Mwansa watched them go, filled with hope for the impact they would make as future custodians of Zambia's cultural legacy. He knew that with their passion and dedication, they would continue to honor and preserve the rich tapestry of Zambia's cultural heritage for generations to come.

Cultural Heritage and Preservation in Zambia

The lecture hall hummed with anticipation as Dr. Mwansa delved deeper into the profound significance of cultural heritage and preservation in Zambia. The students, their eyes shining with reverence and curiosity, leaned forward in their seats, eager to uncover the secrets of their nation's cultural legacy.

"Good afternoon, everyone," Dr. Mwansa greeted, his voice echoing with a sense of reverence and admiration. "Today, we continue our exploration of the cultural dimensions of development in Zambia by delving into the importance of cultural heritage preservation."

With a click, the screen illuminated, revealing images of ancient ruins, sacred sites, and intricate artifacts. "Cultural heritage is the embodiment of Zambia's history, traditions, and identity," Dr. Mwansa began. "It encompasses tangible and intangible expressions of human creativity and ingenuity, from archaeological sites and historical monuments to oral traditions and performing arts."

The next slide displayed diagrams depicting the multi-faceted nature of cultural heritage and its significance for national identity and cohesion. "Cultural heritage preservation is not merely about safeguarding relics of the past; it is about nurturing a sense of pride and belonging among future generations," Dr. Mwansa continued. "It is about ensuring that the stories of our ancestors are preserved and shared, enriching our understanding of who we are and where we come from."

A student raised her hand. "How does cultural heritage preservation contribute to sustainable development in Zambia?"

"An excellent question," Dr. Mwansa replied, bringing up a slide highlighting the link between cultural heritage preservation and sustainable development. "Cultural heritage preservation contributes to sustainable development in Zambia by promoting tourism, fostering social cohesion, and supporting economic diversification."

He then displayed images of heritage sites, cultural festivals, and community-based conservation initiatives. "Cultural tourism, for example, provides opportunities for local communities to showcase their heritage, generate income, and create jobs," Dr. Mwansa explained. "Likewise, the preservation of cultural traditions and practices helps strengthen social bonds, promote intergenerational dialogue, and foster a sense of continuity and belonging."

A student in the front row raised his hand. "How can we ensure the sustainable preservation of cultural heritage in Zambia?"

"Ensuring the sustainable preservation of cultural heritage requires a comprehensive and participatory approach that involves collaboration between government, civil society, and local communities," Dr. Mwansa replied, transitioning to a slide showing strategies for cultural heritage preservation. "This includes conducting heritage assessments, developing conservation plans, and implementing sustainable tourism initiatives that respect and protect cultural sites and traditions."

He then displayed graphs showing the positive impact of cultural heritage preservation on local economies and community well-being. "Moreover, promoting education and awareness about the value of cultural heritage, fostering partnerships with international organizations, and integrating cultural heritage into development planning processes can help ensure its long-term sustainability," Dr. Mwansa concluded. "By working together to preserve our cultural heritage, we can build a more vibrant, inclusive, and resilient Zambia for future generations."

As the lecture concluded, Dr. Mwansa left the students with a final thought. "Cultural heritage preservation is not just a duty; it is a privilege and a responsibility. By honoring and protecting our cultural legacy, we can build a future that is rooted in respect, diversity, and unity."

The students left the hall, their hearts filled with a newfound appreciation for the importance of cultural heritage preservation. They understood that by safeguarding their cultural legacy, they could contribute to a more vibrant and resilient Zambia.

Dr. Mwansa watched them go, filled with hope for the impact they would make as future custodians of Zambia's cultural heritage. He knew that with their passion and dedication, they would continue to honor and preserve the rich tapestry of Zambia's cultural legacy for generations to come.

Indigenous Knowledge and Practices in Zambia

The lecture hall was steeped in a sense of reverence as Dr. Mwansa continued his exploration of the cultural dimensions of development in Zambia, focusing now on the invaluable role of indigenous knowledge and practices. The students, their eyes shining with curiosity and respect, leaned forward in their seats, eager to delve into the wisdom passed down through generations.

"Good afternoon, everyone," Dr. Mwansa greeted, his voice infused with admiration and reverence. "Today, we delve into the rich tapestry of indigenous knowledge and practices that have sustained communities across Zambia for centuries."

With a click, the screen illuminated, revealing images of elders sharing stories, traditional healers practicing their craft, and artisans crafting intricate works of art. "Indigenous knowledge is the accumulated wisdom of generations," Dr. Mwansa began. "It encompasses the traditional practices, beliefs, and values that have sustained communities in harmony with their environment for millennia."

The next slide displayed diagrams depicting the diverse array of indigenous knowledge systems present in Zambia and their relevance to contemporary challenges. "Indigenous knowledge is not static; it evolves and adapts to changing circumstances," Dr. Mwansa continued. "It offers unique insights into sustainable agriculture, natural resource management, and community resilience, providing valuable lessons for modern development."

A student raised her hand. "How can we integrate indigenous knowledge into development initiatives in Zambia?"

"An excellent question," Dr. Mwansa replied, bringing up a slide highlighting strategies for integrating indigenous knowledge into development initiatives. "Integrating indigenous knowledge into development requires recognizing its value, respecting the rights and autonomy of indigenous communities, and fostering partnerships based on mutual respect and collaboration."

He then displayed images of community-led projects, participatory research initiatives, and knowledge exchange programs. "By engaging with indigenous communities as partners and co-creators of knowledge, we can harness the wisdom of traditional practices to address contemporary challenges," Dr. Mwansa explained. "This includes promoting traditional agroecological practices, revitalizing indigenous languages and cultural traditions, and supporting indigenous-led conservation efforts."

A student in the front row raised his hand. "How can we ensure the protection and preservation of indigenous knowledge in Zambia?"

"Ensuring the protection and preservation of indigenous knowledge requires legal recognition, cultural respect, and community empowerment," Dr. Mwansa replied, transitioning to a slide showing strategies for safeguarding indigenous knowledge. "This includes enacting laws and policies that protect traditional knowledge, promoting documentation and archiving initiatives, and providing support for indigenous-led research and education programs."

He then displayed graphs showing the positive impact of integrating indigenous knowledge into development initiatives on community well-being and environmental sustainability. "Moreover, promoting intercultural dialogue and exchange, fostering partnerships between indigenous and scientific knowledge systems, and empowering indigenous communities to lead their own development processes can help ensure the continued vitality and relevance of indigenous knowledge in Zambia," Dr. Mwansa concluded. "By honoring and respecting indigenous knowledge, we can build a more inclusive, equitable, and sustainable future for all."

As the lecture concluded, Dr. Mwansa left the students with a final thought. "Indigenous knowledge is not just a relic of the past; it is a living legacy that holds the key to a more harmonious relationship between humanity and the natural world. By embracing and honoring indigenous knowledge, we can pave the way for a future that is rooted in respect, wisdom, and resilience."

The students left the hall, their minds buzzing with new-found appreciation for the wisdom of their ancestors. They understood that by integrating indigenous knowledge into development initiatives, they could contribute to a more sustainable and equitable Zambia.

Dr. Mwansa watched them go, filled with hope for the impact they would make as future custodians of Zambia's indigenous knowledge. He knew that with their passion and dedication, they would continue to honor and preserve the wisdom of their ancestors for generations to come.

Cultural Globalization and Zambia's Identity

The lecture hall buzzed with anticipation as Dr. Mwansa delved into the complex interplay between cultural globalization and Zambia's identity. The students, their expressions a mix of curiosity and contemplation, leaned forward in their seats, eager to unravel the intricate dynamics shaping their nation's cultural landscape.

"Good afternoon, everyone," Dr. Mwansa greeted, his voice carrying a blend of concern and fascination. "Today, we explore the impact of cultural globalization on Zambia's rich and diverse cultural identity."

With a click, the screen illuminated, revealing images of bustling city streets, vibrant markets, and global media influences. "Cultural globalization refers to the interconnectedness of cultures around the world, driven by advancements in communication, technology, and trade," Dr. Mwansa began. "In Zambia, as in many other nations, cultural globalization presents both opportunities and challenges for the preservation and promotion of our unique cultural heritage."

The next slide displayed diagrams depicting the multi-faceted nature of cultural globalization and its influence on Zambia's cultural identity. "On one hand, cultural globalization has facilitated the exchange of ideas, values, and traditions, enriching our cultural landscape and fostering greater intercultural understanding," Dr. Mwansa continued. "On the other hand, it has also led to the homogenization of culture, the erosion of traditional practices, and the marginalization of indigenous knowledge."

A student raised her hand. "How does cultural globalization impact Zambia's traditional practices and values?"

"An excellent question," Dr. Mwansa replied, bringing up a slide highlighting the impact of cultural globalization on Zambia's traditional practices and values. "Cultural globalization has brought both new opportunities and challenges to Zambia's traditional practices and values. On one hand, it has provided greater access to global markets, technologies, and ideas, enabling cultural exchange and innovation. On the other hand, it has also led to the commodification and commercialization of culture, the loss of traditional knowledge and skills, and the erosion of cultural diversity."

He then displayed images of traditional ceremonies, modern media, and global brands. "For example, while traditional ceremonies such as the Kuomboka may still be celebrated, they are increasingly influenced by modern trends and globalized media," Dr. Mwansa explained. "Likewise, while traditional crafts and arts continue to be practiced, they may face competition from mass-produced goods and global brands."

A student in the front row raised his hand. "How can we preserve Zambia's cultural identity in the face of cultural globalization?"

"Preserving Zambia's cultural identity requires a multi-faceted approach that involves both safeguarding traditional practices and embracing cultural diversity," Dr. Mwansa replied, transitioning to a slide showing strategies for preserving Zambia's cultural identity. "This includes promoting cultural education and awareness, supporting community-based initiatives for cultural preservation, and fostering intercultural dialogue and exchange."

He then displayed graphs showing the positive impact of cultural preservation efforts on community well-being and social cohesion. "Moreover, promoting policies and programs that recognize and support the diversity of cultural expressions, empowering marginalized groups to participate in cultural decision-making processes, and fostering partnerships between government, civil society, and local communities can help ensure the continued vitality and resilience of Zambia's cultural identity," Dr. Mwansa concluded. "By embracing our cultural heritage and celebrating our diversity, we can build a more inclusive, vibrant, and resilient Zambia for future generations."

As the lecture concluded, Dr. Mwansa left the students with a final thought. "Cultural globalization may be inevitable, but its impact on Zambia's cultural identity is not predetermined. By embracing our cultural heritage and celebrating our diversity, we can shape a future that is rooted in respect, dignity, and unity."

The students left the hall, their minds buzzing with new-found insights into the complexities of cultural globalization. They understood that by preserving Zambia's cultural identity, they could contribute to a more vibrant and inclusive society.

Dr. Mwansa watched them go, filled with hope for the impact they would make as future stewards of Zambia's cultural heritage. He knew that with their passion and dedication, they would continue to honor and celebrate the richness and diversity of Zambia's cultural identity for generations to come.

Identity, Diversity, and Inclusion in Zambia

The lecture hall brimmed with anticipation as Dr. Mwansa delved into the intricate tapestry of identity, diversity, and inclusion in Zambia. The students, their faces a mosaic of curiosity and contemplation, leaned forward in their seats, eager to explore the nuanced dynamics shaping their nation's social fabric.

"Good afternoon, everyone," Dr. Mwansa greeted, his voice resonating with a blend of empathy and enthusiasm. "Today, we embark on a journey into the heart of Zambia's identity, celebrating the richness of our diversity and exploring the importance of inclusion in our collective journey towards development."

With a click, the screen illuminated, revealing images of people from diverse ethnicities, cultures, and backgrounds coming together in unity and harmony. "Identity is the essence of who we are, encompassing our ethnicity, culture, language, religion, and values," Dr. Mwansa began. "In Zambia, our identity is as diverse and vibrant as the landscape that surrounds us, reflecting centuries of interaction, exchange, and coexistence."

The next slide displayed diagrams depicting the multi-faceted nature of identity and the importance of embracing diversity and inclusion. "Our diversity is our strength, enriching our society with a tapestry of languages, traditions, and perspectives," Dr. Mwansa continued. "But diversity alone is not enough. Inclusion is the key to unlocking the full potential of our diverse society, ensuring that every individual has a voice, a place, and an opportunity to thrive."

A student raised her hand. "How can we promote inclusion and celebrate diversity in Zambia?"

"An excellent question," Dr. Mwansa replied, bringing up a slide highlighting strategies for promoting inclusion and celebrating diversity. "Promoting inclusion and celebrating diversity requires a concerted effort to challenge stereotypes, address discrimination, and create spaces for dialogue and collaboration."

He then displayed images of community events, cultural festivals, and inclusive initiatives. "It begins with education and awareness, fostering empathy and understanding, and promoting intercultural dialogue and exchange," Dr. Mwansa explained. "It also involves creating policies and programs that recognize and respect the rights and dignity of all individuals, regardless of their background or identity."

A student in the front row raised his hand. "How can we ensure that marginalized groups are included and empowered in Zambia?"

"Ensuring the inclusion and empowerment of marginalized groups requires targeted interventions, affirmative action, and a commitment to social justice," Dr. Mwansa replied, transitioning to a slide showing strategies for promoting inclusion and empowerment. "This includes addressing systemic barriers and inequalities, providing access to education, healthcare, and economic opportunities, and amplifying the voices of marginalized communities in decision-making processes."

He then displayed graphs showing the positive impact of inclusive policies and programs on community well-being and social cohesion. "Moreover, promoting diversity and inclusion not only strengthens social cohesion and resilience but also fosters creativity, innovation, and economic prosperity," Dr. Mwansa concluded. "By embracing our diversity and promoting inclusion, we can build a more equitable, vibrant, and resilient Zambia for future generations."

As the lecture concluded, Dr. Mwansa left the students with a final thought. "Identity, diversity, and inclusion are not just words; they are the foundation of our shared humanity. By celebrating our differences and working together in solidarity, we can build a future that is rooted in respect, dignity, and unity."

The students left the hall, their minds buzzing with newfound insights into the power of diversity and inclusion. They understood that by embracing their diverse identities and promoting inclusion, they could contribute to a more just and compassionate society.

Dr. Mwansa watched them go, filled with hope for the impact they would make as future champions of diversity and inclusion in Zambia. He knew that with their passion and dedication, they would continue to celebrate the richness and diversity of Zambia's identity, fostering a culture of belonging and acceptance for generations to come.

Arts and Creative Industries in Zambia

The lecture hall buzzed with excitement as Dr. Mwansa delved into the vibrant world of arts and creative industries in Zambia. The students, their faces alive with curiosity and enthusiasm, leaned forward in their seats, eager to explore the boundless creativity and cultural richness of their nation.

"Good afternoon, everyone," Dr. Mwansa greeted, his voice infused with passion and admiration. "Today, we embark on a journey into the heart of Zambia's arts and creative industries, celebrating the ingenuity, talent, and diversity of our cultural expression."

With a click, the screen illuminated, revealing images of colorful paintings, intricate sculptures, and captivating performances. "Arts and creative industries are the lifeblood of Zambia's cultural landscape, reflecting the creativity, resilience, and spirit of our people," Dr. Mwansa began. "From traditional crafts and music to contemporary art and film, our creative industries encompass a rich tapestry of expression and innovation."

The next slide displayed diagrams depicting the multifaceted nature of arts and creative industries and their impact on Zambia's cultural and economic development. "Arts and creative industries not only enrich our cultural heritage but also drive economic growth, job creation, and social cohesion," Dr. Mwansa continued. "They provide opportunities for artists, artisans, and cultural entrepreneurs to showcase their talents, generate income, and contribute to the vibrancy of our society."

A student raised her hand. "How can we support and promote the arts and creative industries in Zambia?"

"An excellent question," Dr. Mwansa replied, bringing up a slide highlighting strategies for supporting and promoting the arts and creative industries. "Supporting and promoting the arts and creative industries requires a holistic approach that involves investing in infrastructure, education, and market access."

He then displayed images of art galleries, cultural centers, and creative hubs. "It begins with providing access to training, resources, and networking opportunities for artists and cultural entrepreneurs," Dr. Mwansa explained. "It also involves creating platforms for showcasing and promoting Zambian talent, both domestically and internationally, and fostering partnerships between government, civil society, and the private sector."

A student in the front row raised his hand. "How can the arts and creative industries contribute to social and economic development in Zambia?"

"The arts and creative industries have the potential to drive social and economic development in Zambia by creating jobs, stimulating tourism, and promoting cultural exchange and dialogue," Dr. Mwansa replied, transitioning to a slide showing examples of the impact of the arts and creative industries on development.

He then displayed graphs showing the positive economic impact of the arts and creative industries on local economies and communities. "Moreover, the arts and creative industries play a crucial role in fostering social cohesion, promoting intercultural understanding, and empowering marginalized groups," Dr. Mwansa concluded. "By investing in the arts and creative industries, we can harness the power of culture to build a more inclusive, vibrant, and resilient Zambia for future generations."

As the lecture concluded, Dr. Mwansa left the students with a final thought. "The arts and creative industries are not just about entertainment; they are a reflection of who we are as a society. By supporting and promoting Zambian talent, we can celebrate our cultural heritage and build a future that is rooted in creativity, diversity, and innovation."

The students left the hall, their hearts brimming with inspiration and appreciation for the arts and creative industries. They understood that by embracing their cultural expression and supporting local talent, they could contribute to a more vibrant and prosperous Zambia.

Dr. Mwansa watched them go, filled with hope for the impact they would make as future champions of the arts and creative industries in Zambia. He knew that with their passion and dedication, they would continue to celebrate the richness and diversity of Zambia's cultural expression, enriching the lives of all who call this beautiful country home.

8

Chapter 8: Global Health and Development

Health Systems and Infrastructure in Zambia

The lecture hall fell silent as Dr. Mwansa stepped up to the podium, ready to delve into the intricate realm of global health and development, with a particular focus on Zambia's health systems and infrastructure. The students, their faces reflecting a mix of anticipation and concern, leaned in, eager to grasp the complexities of this vital topic.

"Good afternoon, everyone," Dr. Mwansa greeted, his voice carrying a tone of gravitas and compassion. "Today, we embark on a journey into the realm of global health and development, exploring the challenges and opportunities faced by Zambia's health systems and infrastructure."

With a click, the screen illuminated, revealing images of bustling hospitals, dedicated healthcare workers, and communities striving for better health outcomes. "Health systems and infrastructure are the backbone of any society, providing essential services and support to ensure the well-being of its citizens," Dr. Mwansa began. "In Zambia, as in many other countries, the state of our health systems and infrastructure plays a critical role in determining the health outcomes and quality of life of our people."

The next slide displayed diagrams depicting the various components of Zambia's health systems and infrastructure, from healthcare facilities and medical equipment to healthcare financing and human resources. "Our health systems and infrastructure face numerous challenges, including inadequate funding, limited access to essential services, and a shortage of skilled healthcare workers," Dr. Mwansa continued. "These challenges are further exacerbated by factors such as geographic disparities, demographic shifts, and the burden of disease."

A student raised her hand. "How can we strengthen Zambia's health systems and infrastructure to improve health outcomes?"

"An excellent question," Dr. Mwansa replied, bringing up a slide highlighting strategies for strengthening Zambia's health systems and infrastructure. "Strengthening Zambia's health systems and infrastructure requires a comprehensive approach that addresses the underlying determinants of health, improves access to essential services, and enhances the quality of care."

He then displayed images of healthcare training programs, medical supply chains, and community health initiatives. "It begins with increasing investment in healthcare infrastructure, including the construction and renovation of healthcare facilities, the procurement of medical equipment and supplies, and the expansion of healthcare services to underserved areas," Dr. Mwansa explained. "It also involves investing in the training and retention of healthcare workers, strengthening health information systems, and promoting community engagement and empowerment."

A student in the front row raised his hand. "How can we ensure that Zambia's health systems and infrastructure are resilient and adaptable to future challenges?"

"Ensuring the resilience and adaptability of Zambia's health systems and infrastructure requires ongoing monitoring, evaluation, and adaptation," Dr. Mwansa replied, transitioning to a slide showing examples of resilient health systems. "This includes strengthening disease surveillance and response mechanisms, building partnerships with other sectors, such as education and agriculture, and integrating innovations in technology and telemedicine."

He then displayed graphs showing the positive impact of resilient health systems on health outcomes and community well-being. "Moreover, promoting equity, sustainability, and community participation in health planning and decision-making processes can help ensure that Zambia's health systems and infrastructure are responsive to the needs of all citizens," Dr. Mwansa concluded. "By working together to strengthen our health systems and infrastructure, we can build a healthier, more resilient Zambia for future generations."

As the lecture concluded, Dr. Mwansa left the students with a final thought. "Health is not just the absence of disease; it is a fundamental human right. By investing in our health systems and infrastructure, we can create a future where every Zambian has the opportunity to lead a healthy and fulfilling life."

The students left the hall, their minds buzzing with new-found insights into the importance of health systems and infrastructure in shaping the well-being of communities. They understood that by working together to strengthen Zambia's health systems and infrastructure, they could contribute to a healthier, more prosperous future for all.

Dr. Mwansa watched them go, filled with hope for the impact they would make as future leaders and advocates for health and development in Zambia. He knew that with their passion and dedication, they would continue to strive towards a future where every Zambian has access to the care and support they need to thrive.

Disease Prevention and Control in Zambia

The atmosphere in the lecture hall shifted as Dr. Mwansa prepared to delve into the critical topic of disease prevention and control in Zambia. The students, their expressions a mix of solemnity and determination, braced themselves for an exploration of the challenges and strategies in combating diseases within their nation.

"Good afternoon, everyone," Dr. Mwansa greeted, his voice carrying a weight of urgency and resolve. "Today, we confront the pressing issue of disease prevention and control in Zambia, a vital aspect of global health and development."

With a click, the screen illuminated, revealing images of medical teams administering vaccines, community health workers conducting outreach programs, and individuals practicing hygiene measures. "Disease prevention and control are fundamental pillars of public health, aimed at reducing the burden of communicable and non-communicable diseases,"

Dr. Mwansa began. "In Zambia, as in many other countries, the prevention and control of diseases are paramount for safeguarding the health and well-being of our population."

The next slide displayed diagrams illustrating the prevalence of various diseases in Zambia, from malaria and HIV/AIDS to tuberculosis and non-communicable diseases. "Zambia faces a multitude of health challenges, including infectious diseases such as malaria, HIV/AIDS, and tuberculosis, as well as non-communicable diseases like diabetes, hypertension, and cancer," Dr. Mwansa continued. "These diseases not only impose a heavy burden on individuals and families but also strain our healthcare systems and hinder our socio-economic development."

A student raised her hand. "How can we improve disease prevention and control efforts in Zambia?"

"An excellent question," Dr. Mwansa replied, bringing up a slide highlighting strategies for enhancing disease prevention and control efforts. "Improving disease prevention and control in Zambia requires a comprehensive approach that addresses both the determinants of health and the specific challenges posed by different diseases."

He then displayed images of community health education campaigns, vector control programs, and vaccination drives. "It begins with promoting health education and behavior change, raising awareness about the importance of preventive measures such as vaccination, mosquito nets, and safe hygiene practices," Dr. Mwansa explained. "It also involves strengthening disease surveillance and response systems, improving access to essential medicines and diagnostics, and fostering collaboration between government, civil society, and international partners."

A student in the front row raised his hand. "How can we ensure that disease prevention and control efforts are sustainable and effective in the long term?"

"Ensuring the sustainability and effectiveness of disease prevention and control efforts requires a holistic approach that addresses the underlying determinants of health, builds community resilience, and fosters partnerships for health," Dr. Mwansa replied, transitioning to a slide showing examples of sustainable disease prevention and control initiatives. "This includes investing in primary healthcare infrastructure, empowering communities to take ownership of their health, and integrating disease prevention and control into broader development agendas."

He then displayed graphs showing the positive impact of sustainable disease prevention and control efforts on health outcomes and community well-being. "Moreover, promoting equity, social justice, and human rights in health policies and programs can help ensure that disease prevention and control efforts reach those who need them most," Dr. Mwansa concluded. "By working together to strengthen our disease prevention and control efforts, we can build a healthier, more resilient Zambia for future generations."

As the lecture concluded, Dr. Mwansa left the students with a final thought. "Disease prevention and control are not just about treating illnesses; they are about promoting health and saving lives. By investing in preventive measures and fostering collaboration, we can create a future where every Zambian has the opportunity to live a healthy and fulfilling life."

The students left the hall, their minds buzzing with new-found insights into the importance of disease prevention and control in promoting public health. They understood that by working together to enhance disease prevention and control efforts, they could contribute to a healthier, more prosperous Zambia for all.

Dr. Mwansa watched them go, filled with hope for the impact they would make as future leaders and advocates for health and development in Zambia. He knew that with their passion and dedication, they would continue to strive towards a future where diseases are prevented, lives are saved, and communities thrive.

Access to Healthcare and Equity in Zambia

The air in the lecture hall thickened with anticipation as Dr. Mwansa prepared to delve into the critical topic of access to healthcare and equity in Zambia. The students, their faces a blend of concern and determination, leaned forward in their seats, ready to confront the challenges and disparities within their nation's healthcare system.

"Good afternoon, everyone," Dr. Mwansa greeted, his voice carrying a tone of empathy and resolve. "Today, we confront the pressing issue of access to healthcare and equity in Zambia, a fundamental aspect of global health and development."

With a click, the screen illuminated, revealing images of bustling clinics, remote healthcare outposts, and individuals seeking medical care. "Access to healthcare is a basic human right, essential for achieving good health and well-being," Dr. Mwansa began. "In Zambia, as in many other countries, ensuring equitable access to healthcare is paramount for addressing health disparities and promoting social justice."

The next slide displayed diagrams illustrating the disparities in healthcare access across different regions and population groups in Zambia. "Zambia faces significant challenges in ensuring equitable access to healthcare, with disparities in access persisting across geographic, socioeconomic, and demographic lines," Dr. Mwansa continued. "Rural and remote areas often lack adequate healthcare infrastructure and services, while vulnerable populations such as women, children, and people living with disabilities face barriers to accessing essential care."

A student raised her hand. "How can we improve access to healthcare and promote equity in Zambia?"

"An excellent question," Dr. Mwansa replied, bringing up a slide highlighting strategies for enhancing access to healthcare and promoting equity. "Improving access to healthcare and promoting equity in Zambia requires a multi-faceted approach that addresses both supply-side and demand-side barriers to care."

He then displayed images of mobile clinics, community health workers, and health financing schemes. "It begins with strengthening primary healthcare infrastructure and expanding healthcare services to underserved areas," Dr. Mwansa explained. "It also involves promoting community-based healthcare initiatives, investing in the training and deployment of frontline healthcare workers, and implementing policies to address financial barriers to care, such as user fees and health insurance."

A student in the front row raised his hand. "How can we ensure that vulnerable populations have equitable access to healthcare?"

"Ensuring equitable access to healthcare for vulnerable populations requires targeted interventions and affirmative action," Dr. Mwansa replied, transitioning to a slide showing examples of programs targeting vulnerable populations. "This includes prioritizing the needs of vulnerable populations in healthcare planning and resource allocation, implementing targeted health promotion and outreach programs, and addressing social determinants of health such as poverty, gender inequality, and discrimination."

He then displayed graphs showing the positive impact of equitable access to healthcare on health outcomes and community well-being. "Moreover, promoting equity in healthcare requires addressing systemic barriers and inequalities, advocating for policies that prioritize the needs of marginalized groups, and fostering partnerships between government, civil society, and communities," Dr. Mwansa concluded. "By working together to ensure equitable access to healthcare, we can build a healthier, more inclusive Zambia for all."

As the lecture concluded, Dr. Mwansa left the students with a final thought. "Access to healthcare is not just about providing medical treatment; it is about upholding human dignity and promoting social justice. By advocating for equitable access to healthcare, we can create a future where every Zambian has the opportunity to lead a healthy and fulfilling life."

The students left the hall, their minds buzzing with newfound insights into the importance of access to healthcare and equity in promoting public health. They understood that by working together to address disparities and barriers to care, they could contribute to a healthier, more equitable Zambia for all.

Dr. Mwansa watched them go, filled with hope for the impact they would make as future leaders and advocates for health and development in Zambia. He knew that with their passion and dedication, they would continue to strive towards a future where access to healthcare is a reality for every Zambian, regardless of their circumstances.

Nutrition and Food Security in Zambia

The lecture hall buzzed with anticipation as Dr. Mwansa prepared to explore the critical topic of nutrition and food security in Zambia. The students, their faces a mixture of concern and determination, leaned in, eager to understand the complexities surrounding access to adequate nutrition and food within their nation.

"Good afternoon, everyone," Dr. Mwansa greeted, his voice projecting a blend of empathy and urgency. "Today, we confront the pressing issue of nutrition and food security in Zambia, a fundamental aspect of global health and development."

With a click, the screen illuminated, revealing images of fertile farmlands, bustling markets, and families gathering around the dinner table. "Nutrition and food security are essential for ensuring the health and well-being of individuals and communities," Dr. Mwansa began. "In Zambia, as in many other countries, access to nutritious food is a cornerstone of public health and socioeconomic development."

The next slide displayed diagrams illustrating the factors influencing nutrition and food security in Zambia, from agricultural production and distribution to household food consumption patterns. "Zambia faces significant challenges in ensuring nutrition and food security for all its citizens, with disparities in access to nutritious food persisting across rural and urban areas, as well as among different socioeconomic groups," Dr. Mwansa continued. "Malnutrition, both under-nutrition and overnutrition, poses a dual burden, affecting individuals and communities across the lifespan."

A student raised her hand. "How can we improve nutrition and food security in Zambia?"

"An excellent question," Dr. Mwansa replied, bringing up a slide highlighting strategies for enhancing nutrition and food security. "Improving nutrition and food security in Zambia requires a comprehensive approach that addresses both the availability and accessibility of nutritious food, as well as the underlying determinants of food insecurity."

He then displayed images of agricultural diversification, nutrition education programs, and food fortification initiatives. "It begins with promoting sustainable agricultural practices and increasing the availability of diverse, nutrient-rich foods," Dr. Mwansa explained. "It also involves addressing poverty and inequality, improving access to clean water and sanitation, and empowering communities to make healthy food choices."

A student in the front row raised his hand. "How can we ensure that vulnerable populations, such as children and pregnant women, have access to adequate nutrition?"

"Ensuring access to adequate nutrition for vulnerable pop-ulations requires targeted interventions and support," Dr. Mwansa replied, transitioning to a slide showing examples of programs targeting vulnerable groups. "This includes implementing nutrition-sensitive programs that address the unique needs of children, pregnant women, and lactating mothers, as well as promoting breastfeeding, micronutrient supplementation, and early childhood nutrition."

He then displayed graphs showing the positive impact of

improved nutrition and food security on health outcomes and community well-being. "Moreover, promoting food sovereignty, resilience, and sustainability can help build a more resilient food system that can withstand shocks and crises," Dr. Mwansa concluded. "By working together to improve nutrition and food security, we can build a healthier, more prosperous Zambia for future generations."

As the lecture concluded, Dr. Mwansa left the students with a final thought. "Nutrition and food security are not just about filling stomachs; they are about nourishing bodies and minds. By investing in nutritious food and sustainable food systems, we can create a future where every Zambian has access to the nourishment they need to thrive."

The students left the hall, their minds buzzing with new-found insights into the importance of nutrition and food security in promoting public health. They understood that by working together to address food insecurity and malnutrition, they could contribute to a healthier, more resilient Zambia for all.

Dr. Mwansa watched them go, filled with hope for the impact they would make as future leaders and advocates for nutrition and food security in Zambia. He knew that with their passion and dedication, they would continue to strive towards a future where nutritious food is a reality for every Zambian, ensuring a healthier, more prosperous nation for generations to come.

Mental Health and Well-Being in Zambia

The atmosphere in the lecture hall shifted as Dr. Mwansa prepared to delve into the crucial topic of mental health and well-being in Zambia. The students, their faces reflecting a mix of solemnity and concern, braced themselves for an exploration of the challenges and stigma surrounding mental health within their nation.

"Good afternoon, everyone," Dr. Mwansa greeted, his voice carrying a tone of compassion and understanding. "Today, we confront the pressing issue of mental health and well-being in Zambia, an essential but often overlooked aspect of public health and development."

With a click, the screen illuminated, revealing images of individuals seeking support, mental health professionals providing care, and communities coming together to raise awareness. "Mental health is a fundamental component of overall well-being, affecting individuals, families, and communities," Dr. Mwansa began. "In Zambia, as in many other countries, mental health disorders are prevalent, yet access to care and support remains limited."

The next slide displayed diagrams illustrating the burden of mental health disorders in Zambia, from depression and anxiety to psychosis and substance use disorders. "Zambia faces significant challenges in addressing mental health and well-being, with stigma, discrimination, and a lack of resources hindering efforts to provide adequate care and support," Dr. Mwansa continued. "Mental health disorders not only impact individuals' quality of life but also contribute to social and economic burdens on families and communities."

A student raised her hand. "How can we improve mental

health and well-being in Zambia?"

"An excellent question," Dr. Mwansa replied, bringing up a slide highlighting strategies for enhancing mental health and well-being. "Improving mental health and well-being in Zambia requires a multi-faceted approach that addresses both the prevention and treatment of mental health disorders, as well as the broader social determinants of mental health."

He then displayed images of mental health awareness campaigns, community support groups, and mental health care facilities. "It begins with raising awareness and reducing stigma surrounding mental health, promoting mental health literacy, and encouraging help-seeking behaviors," Dr. Mwansa explained. "It also involves increasing access to mental health services, including counseling, therapy, and psychiatric care, as well as integrating mental health into primary healthcare systems."

A student in the front row raised his hand. "How can we ensure that mental health services are accessible and culturally appropriate for all Zambians?"

"Ensuring accessibility and cultural appropriateness of mental health services requires a person-centered approach and community engagement," Dr. Mwansa replied, transitioning to a slide showing examples of culturally sensitive mental health programs. "This includes training healthcare providers in culturally competent care, involving communities in the design and delivery of mental health services, and addressing barriers to access, such as transportation and affordability."

He then displayed graphs showing the positive impact of improved mental health and well-being on individual and community outcomes. "Moreover, promoting resilience, social support, and self-care can help build individual and community resilience to mental health challenges," Dr. Mwansa concluded. "By working together to improve mental health and well-being, we can create a future where every Zambian has the support and resources they need to thrive."

As the lecture concluded, Dr. Mwansa left the students with a final thought. "Mental health is not just the absence of illness; it is a state of well-being in which individuals can realize their potential, cope with life's challenges, and contribute to their communities. By investing in mental health and well-being, we can create a healthier, more resilient Zambia for future generations."

The students left the hall, their minds buzzing with new-found insights into the importance of mental health and well-being in promoting overall health and development. They understood that by working together to address mental health challenges and stigma, they could contribute to a healthier, more compassionate Zambia for all.

Dr. Mwansa watched them go, filled with hope for the impact they would make as future leaders and advocates for mental health in Zambia. He knew that with their passion and dedication, they would continue to strive towards a future where mental health and well-being are valued, supported, and prioritized.

Global Health Initiatives and Zambia's Participation

The lecture hall hummed with anticipation as Dr. Mwansa prepared to delve into the pivotal topic of global health initiatives and Zambia's participation. The students, their expressions a blend of curiosity and determination, leaned forward in their seats, eager to grasp the intricacies of

Zambia's role in international health efforts.

"Good afternoon, everyone," Dr. Mwansa greeted, his voice resonating with a sense of importance and opportunity. "Today, we explore the vital realm of global health initiatives and Zambia's participation, crucial elements in shaping the health landscape both locally and globally."

With a click, the screen illuminated, revealing images of collaborative projects, international conferences, and health-care workers from diverse backgrounds. "Global health initiatives play a pivotal role in addressing health challenges that transcend national borders, from infectious diseases to non-communicable illnesses," Dr. Mwansa began. "In Zambia, as in many countries, participation in these initiatives offers opportunities for collaboration, capacity-building, and shared learning."

The next slide displayed diagrams illustrating Zambia's involvement in various global health initiatives, from vaccination campaigns to research partnerships. "Zambia actively participates in a range of global health initiatives, contributing expertise, resources, and experiences to international efforts," Dr. Mwansa continued. "Through these collaborations, Zambia not only gains access to vital resources and knowledge but also strengthens its own health systems and capacities."

A student raised her hand. "How does Zambia benefit from its participation in global health initiatives?"

"An excellent question," Dr. Mwansa replied, bringing up a slide highlighting the benefits of Zambia's engagement in global health initiatives. "Zambia benefits from its participation in global health initiatives in numerous ways, including access to funding, technical support, and opportunities for networking and collaboration."

He then displayed images of healthcare workers attending international conferences, receiving training, and implementing best practices learned from global partners. "Participation in global health initiatives also allows Zambia to share its own experiences and expertise, contributing to global health knowledge and strengthening its reputation as a leader in health innovation and implementation," Dr. Mwansa explained. "Moreover, by aligning with international goals and standards, Zambia can attract investment, support, and recognition for its health priorities and achievements."

A student in the front row raised his hand. "How can Zambia further enhance its participation in global health initiatives?"

"Ensuring effective participation in global health initiatives requires strategic planning, coordination, and collaboration," Dr. Mwansa replied, transitioning to a slide showing examples of strategies for enhancing Zambia's engagement. "This includes strengthening partnerships with international organizations, donor agencies, and other stakeholders, as well as leveraging technology and innovation to expand access to health information and services."

He then displayed graphs showing the positive impact of Zambia's participation in global health initiatives on health outcomes and system capacities. "Moreover, advocating for equitable participation and representation in global health governance structures can help ensure that Zambia's voice is heard and its priorities are addressed on the international stage," Dr. Mwansa concluded. "By working together to enhance Zambia's participation in global health initiatives, we can contribute to a healthier, more interconnected world for all."

As the lecture concluded, Dr. Mwansa left the students with

a final thought. "Global health initiatives are not just about addressing health challenges; they are about building partnerships, sharing knowledge, and working together to create a healthier, more equitable world. By actively participating in these initiatives, we can create a future where every Zambian has the opportunity to lead a healthy and fulfilling life."

The students left the hall, their minds buzzing with new-found insights into the importance of Zambia's role in global health initiatives. They understood that by actively engaging in international collaborations, they could contribute to a healthier, more interconnected world, where health knows no borders.

Dr. Mwansa watched them go, filled with hope for the impact they would make as future leaders and advocates for global health in Zambia. He knew that with their passion and dedication, they would continue to strive towards a future where health is a shared priority, both locally and globally.

9

Chapter 9: Education and Development

Access to Education in Zambia

The lecture hall buzzed with anticipation as Dr. Mwansa prepared to explore the pivotal topic of education and development in Zambia. The students, their faces illuminated with curiosity and determination, eagerly awaited insights into the challenges and opportunities surrounding education within their nation.

"Good afternoon, everyone," Dr. Mwansa greeted, his voice resonating with warmth and purpose. "Today, we embark on a journey through the realm of education and development in Zambia, a journey that shapes the future of individuals, communities, and our nation as a whole."

With a click, the screen illuminated, revealing images of bustling classrooms, eager students, and dedicated teachers. "Access to education is a fundamental human right and a cornerstone of development," Dr. Mwansa began. "In Zambia, as in many countries, education serves as a catalyst for social mobility, economic growth, and societal transformation."

The next slide displayed diagrams illustrating the disparities in access to education across different regions and population groups in Zambia, from urban centers to rural villages. "Zambia faces significant challenges in ensuring equitable access to education for all its citizens," Dr. Mwansa continued. "Barriers such as poverty, distance, cultural norms, and gender inequality often limit access to quality education, particularly for marginalized populations."

A student raised her hand. "How can we improve access to education in Zambia?"

"An excellent question," Dr. Mwansa replied, bringing up a slide highlighting strategies for enhancing access to education. "Improving access to education in Zambia requires a multi-faceted approach that addresses both the supply and demand sides of the education equation."

He then displayed images of school infrastructure projects, scholarship programs, and community-based education initiatives. "It begins with investing in educational infrastructure, such as schools, classrooms, and learning materials, to ensure that every child has a safe and conducive environment for learning," Dr. Mwansa explained. "It also involves addressing socio-economic barriers to education, such as poverty and inequality, through targeted interventions such as school feeding programs, cash transfers, and scholarships."

A student in the front row raised her hand. "How can we ensure that marginalized populations, such as girls and children with disabilities, have equal access to education?"

"Ensuring equal access to education for all requires addressing systemic barriers and discrimination," Dr. Mwansa replied, transitioning to a slide showing examples of inclusive education initiatives. "This includes promoting gender equality and empowerment, eliminating school-related gender-based violence, and providing accommodations and support services for children with disabilities."

He then displayed graphs showing the positive impact of improved access to education on individual and societal outcomes. "Moreover, by promoting lifelong learning opportunities and non-formal education programs, we can ensure that education remains accessible and relevant throughout life," Dr. Mwansa concluded. "By working together to improve access to education, we can unlock the full potential of every Zambian and build a brighter future for our nation."

As the lecture concluded, Dr. Mwansa left the students with a final thought. "Education is not just about acquiring knowledge; it is about empowering individuals, transforming communities, and shaping the future. By investing in education, we can create a future where every Zambian has the opportunity to fulfill their potential and contribute to the development of our nation."

The students left the hall, their minds buzzing with new-found insights into the importance of education in driving development and progress. They understood that by working together to expand access to quality education, they could contribute to a brighter, more prosperous future for Zambia.

Dr. Mwansa watched them go, filled with hope for the impact they would make as future leaders and advocates for education and development in Zambia. He knew that with their passion and dedication, they would continue to strive towards a future where education is a right, not a privilege, and where every child has the opportunity to learn, grow, and succeed.

Quality of Education in Zambia

The lecture hall fell into a hushed anticipation as Dr. Mwansa prepared to delve into the critical topic of the quality of education in Zambia. The students, their expressions a mix of concern and determination, leaned forward in their seats, eager to understand the nuances of educational standards within their nation.

"Good afternoon, everyone," Dr. Mwansa greeted, his voice carrying a tone of urgency and resolve. "Today, we confront the pressing issue of the quality of education in Zambia, an essential aspect of fostering individual growth, societal progress, and national development."

With a click, the screen illuminated, revealing images of classrooms filled with eager faces, teachers engaged in instruction, and students immersed in learning activities. "Quality education is not merely about access to schools and classrooms; it is about the caliber of teaching, the relevance of the curriculum, and the outcomes achieved," Dr. Mwansa began. "In Zambia, as in many countries, ensuring high-quality education is paramount for preparing individuals to thrive in an ever-changing world."

The next slide displayed diagrams illustrating the various dimensions of educational quality, from teacher qualifications to learning outcomes. "Zambia faces significant challenges in ensuring the quality of education across its schools and educational institutions," Dr. Mwansa continued. "Issues such as teacher shortages, inadequate training, outdated curricula, and limited resources often impede efforts to provide a high-quality education for all learners."

A student raised her hand. "How can we improve the quality of education in Zambia?"

"An excellent question," Dr. Mwansa replied, bringing up a slide highlighting strategies for enhancing the quality of education. "Improving the quality of education in Zambia requires a comprehensive approach that addresses both the inputs and processes of education, as well as the outcomes and impacts."

He then displayed images of teacher training programs, curriculum reforms, and school infrastructure improvements. "It begins with investing in teacher recruitment, training, and professional development to ensure that educators have the knowledge, skills, and support they need to deliver effective instruction," Dr. Mwansa explained. "It also involves updating and contextualizing the curriculum to reflect the needs and aspirations of Zambian learners, as well as providing adequate resources and facilities to support teaching and learning."

A student in the front row raised his hand. "How can we measure the quality of education in Zambia?"

"Measuring the quality of education requires a combination of quantitative and qualitative indicators," Dr. Mwansa replied, transitioning to a slide showing examples of educational quality assessments. "This includes assessing student learning outcomes through standardized tests, evaluating teaching practices through classroom observations, and gathering feedback from students, parents, and communities."

He then displayed graphs showing the positive impact of improved educational quality on individual achievement and national development. "Moreover, promoting a culture of continuous improvement and accountability can help ensure that educational quality remains a priority for all stakeholders," Dr. Mwansa concluded. "By working together to improve the quality of education, we can equip every Zambian learner with the knowledge, skills, and opportunities they need to succeed."

As the lecture concluded, Dr. Mwansa left the students with a final thought. "Quality education is not just about passing exams; it is about empowering individuals to think critically, solve problems, and contribute meaningfully to society. By investing in the quality of education, we can unlock the full potential of every Zambian learner and build a brighter future for our nation."

The students left the hall, their minds buzzing with new-found insights into the importance of educational quality in driving individual and societal success. They understood that by working together to enhance the quality of education, they could contribute to a more prosperous and equitable Zambia for all.

Dr. Mwansa watched them go, filled with hope for the impact they would make as future leaders and advocates for high-quality education in Zambia. He knew that with their passion and dedication, they would continue to strive towards a future where every learner receives a world-class education, unlocking opportunities for personal growth and national development.

Education and Economic Development in Zambia

The lecture hall brimmed with eager anticipation as Dr. Mwansa prepared to delve into the intricate relationship between education and economic development in Zambia. The students, their faces a portrait of curiosity and determination, leaned forward in their seats, ready to unravel the complexities of this vital connection.

"Good afternoon, everyone," Dr. Mwansa greeted, his voice resonating with a blend of enthusiasm and purpose. "Today, we explore the symbiotic relationship between education and economic development in Zambia, a dynamic interplay that shapes the trajectory of our nation's prosperity and progress."

With a click, the screen illuminated, revealing images of bustling marketplaces, innovative industries, and empowered entrepreneurs. "Education serves as the cornerstone of economic development, providing individuals with the knowledge, skills, and capabilities necessary to thrive in a competitive global economy," Dr. Mwansa began. "In Zambia, as in many countries, investments in education lay the foundation for sustainable economic growth, poverty reduction, and social advancement."

The next slide displayed diagrams illustrating the various ways in which education impacts economic development, from enhancing workforce productivity to fostering innovation and entrepreneurship. "Zambia faces significant challenges in harnessing the full potential of education to drive economic development," Dr. Mwansa continued. "Issues such as skills mismatches, youth unemployment, and disparities in educational access and quality often hinder efforts to leverage education as a catalyst for economic transformation."

A student raised her hand. "How can we maximize the contribution of education to economic development in Zambia?"

"An excellent question," Dr. Mwansa replied, bringing up a slide highlighting strategies for enhancing the link between education and economic development. "Maximizing the contribution of education to economic development requires a holistic approach that addresses both the supply and demand sides of the education-economy nexus."

He then displayed images of vocational training programs, industry-academic partnerships, and entrepreneurship initiatives. "It begins with aligning educational curricula and training programs with the needs of the labor market, ensuring that learners acquire relevant skills and competencies that are in demand by employers," Dr. Mwansa explained. "It also involves promoting lifelong learning, innovation, and digital literacy to equip individuals with the adaptability and resilience needed to thrive in a rapidly changing economic landscape."

A student in the front row raised his hand. "How can education contribute to inclusive economic development in Zambia?"

"Education plays a critical role in fostering inclusive economic development by expanding opportunities for all individuals, regardless of their background or circumstances," Dr. Mwansa replied, transitioning to a slide showing examples of inclusive education and economic empowerment initiatives. "This includes promoting gender equality, empowering marginalized groups, and providing targeted support to vulnerable populations to ensure that everyone can participate in and benefit from economic opportunities."

He then displayed graphs showing the positive impact of education on various edous economic indicators, from GDP growth to income inequality reduction. "Moreover, investing in education not only yields economic dividends but also contributes to broader social and human development goals, including improved health outcomes, reduced poverty, and increased social cohesion," Dr. Mwansa concluded. "By working together to harness the power of education for economic development, we can build a more prosperous, equitable, and resilient Zambia for all."

As the lecture concluded, Dr. Mwansa left the students with a final thought. "Education is not just a means to an end; it is a powerful driver of economic transformation and societal progress. By investing in education, we invest in the future of our nation, unlocking opportunities for growth, innovation, and prosperity."

The students left the hall, their minds buzzing with new-found insights into the transformative potential of education in driving economic development. They understood that by working together to strengthen the link between education and the economy, they could contribute to a brighter, more prosperous future for Zambia.

Dr. Mwansa watched them go, filled with hope for the impact they would make as future leaders and innovators in Zambia's journey towards economic prosperity. He knew that with their passion, determination, and commitment to education, they would continue to drive progress and positive change, shaping a future where every Zambian has the opportunity to thrive.

Lifelong Learning and Skills Development in Zambia

The lecture hall hummed with anticipation as Dr. Mwansa prepared to explore the transformative power of lifelong learning and skills development in Zambia. The students, their faces illuminated with curiosity and determination, eagerly awaited insights into how continuous learning could shape their futures.

"Good afternoon, everyone," Dr. Mwansa greeted, his voice carrying a tone of excitement and possibility. "Today, we embark on a journey through the realm of lifelong learning and skills development in Zambia, a journey that holds the key to personal growth, professional advancement, and national prosperity."

With a click, the screen illuminated, revealing images of individuals engaged in diverse learning activities, from traditional classrooms to vocational training workshops. "Lifelong learning is more than just acquiring qualifications; it is a mindset, a commitment to continuous growth and development throughout life," Dr. Mwansa began. "In Zambia, as in many countries, lifelong learning plays a crucial role in equipping individuals with the knowledge, skills, and competencies needed to navigate a rapidly changing world."

The next slide displayed diagrams illustrating the various dimensions of lifelong learning, from formal education to informal learning opportunities. "Zambia faces significant challenges in promoting lifelong learning and skills development across its population," Dr. Mwansa continued. "Issues such as limited access to educational opportunities, outdated training programs, and inadequate support for adult learners often hinder efforts to foster a culture of lifelong learning."

A student raised her hand. "How can we promote lifelong learning and skills development in Zambia?"

"An excellent question," Dr. Mwansa replied, bringing up a slide highlighting strategies for enhancing lifelong learning and skills development. "Promoting lifelong learning and skills development requires a multi-faceted approach that addresses both the individual and systemic barriers to learning."

He then displayed images of adult education programs, skills training initiatives, and digital learning platforms. "It begins with expanding access to flexible and affordable learning opportunities, such as adult education programs, vocational training courses, and online learning platforms, to cater to the diverse needs and interests of learners," Dr. Mwansa explained. "It also involves promoting a culture of innovation and entrepreneurship, empowering individuals to adapt to new technologies and market trends."

A student in the front row raised her hand. "How can lifelong learning contribute to personal and professional development?"

"Lifelong learning offers individuals the opportunity to acquire new skills, explore new interests, and pursue new career pathways throughout their lives," Dr. Mwansa replied, transitioning to a slide showing examples of lifelong learning benefits. "By continuously updating their knowledge and skills, individuals can remain competitive in the job market, enhance their earning potential, and pursue fulfilling career opportunities."

He then displayed graphs showing the positive impact of life-long learning on various indicators, from employment rates to job satisfaction. "Moreover, lifelong learning fosters personal growth, self-confidence, and social inclusion, empowering individuals to contribute meaningfully to their communities and society as a whole," Dr. Mwansa concluded. "By working together to promote lifelong learning and skills development, we can unlock the full potential of every Zambian and build a more prosperous and resilient nation."

As the lecture concluded, Dr. Mwansa left the students with a final thought. "Lifelong learning is not just about acquiring qualifications; it is about embracing opportunities, pursuing passions, and realizing potential. By investing in lifelong learning and skills development, we invest in the future of our nation, unlocking possibilities for personal fulfillment, economic growth, and social progress."

The students left the hall, their minds buzzing with new-found insights into the importance of lifelong learning in shaping their futures. They understood that by embracing a mindset of continuous growth and development, they could navigate the complexities of the modern world and seize opportunities for success.

Dr. Mwansa watched them go, filled with hope for the impact they would make as lifelong learners and contributors to Zambia's journey towards prosperity. He knew that with their passion, determination, and commitment to lifelong learning, they would continue to drive progress and positive change, shaping a future where every Zambian has the opportunity to thrive.

Technology in Education in Zambia

The lecture hall buzzed with excitement as Dr. Mwansa prepared to delve into the transformative role of technology in education within Zambia. The students, their faces lit up with anticipation, leaned forward in their seats, eager to explore the possibilities that technology could offer to enhance learning experiences.

"Good afternoon, everyone," Dr. Mwansa greeted, his voice carrying a tone of enthusiasm and optimism. "Today, we embark on a journey through the realm of technology in education in Zambia, a journey that holds the promise of revolutionizing teaching and learning."

With a click, the screen illuminated, revealing images of digital classrooms, interactive learning platforms, and students engaging with technology-enhanced educational resources. "Technology has the power to democratize access to education, personalize learning experiences, and prepare learners for the demands of the 21st century," Dr. Mwansa began. "In Zambia, as in many countries, the integration of technology into education holds the potential to overcome traditional barriers to learning and empower individuals with the skills and knowledge they need to thrive in a digital world."

The next slide displayed diagrams illustrating the various ways in which technology can enhance education, from facilitating remote learning to enabling personalized instruction. "Zambia faces significant challenges in harnessing the full potential of technology in education," Dr. Mwansa continued. "Issues such as limited access to digital infrastructure, inadequate teacher training, and digital literacy gaps among learners often hinder efforts to leverage technology for educational purposes."

A student raised her hand. "How can we maximize the benefits of technology in education in Zambia?"

"An excellent question," Dr. Mwansa replied, bringing up a slide highlighting strategies for integrating technology into education. "Maximizing the benefits of technology in education requires a comprehensive approach that addresses both the technical and pedagogical aspects of technology integration."

He then displayed images of teacher training workshops, digital literacy programs, and initiatives to expand access to digital devices and connectivity. "It begins with investing in digital infrastructure and providing teachers and students with the training and support they need to effectively use technology for teaching and learning," Dr. Mwansa explained. "It also involves developing digital educational resources and platforms that are culturally relevant, accessible, and engaging for learners."

A student in the front row raised her hand. "How can technology help address the challenges of access to education in remote and underserved areas of Zambia?"

"Technology has the potential to bridge the geographic divide and bring quality education to even the most remote and underserved communities," Dr. Mwansa replied, transitioning to a slide showing examples of technology-enabled education initiatives. "By leveraging online learning platforms, mobile devices, and satellite connectivity, we can provide learners in remote areas with access to educational resources, interactive lessons, and virtual classrooms."

He then displayed graphs showing the positive impact of technology in education on various indicators, from academic achievement to educational equity. "Moreover, technology can empower learners to take ownership of their learning, foster collaboration and creativity, and prepare them for the demands of the digital economy," Dr. Mwansa concluded. "By working together to harness the power of technology in education, we can build a more inclusive, innovative, and resilient education system for Zambia."

As the lecture concluded, Dr. Mwansa left the students with a final thought. "Technology is not a panacea, but it is a powerful tool for advancing education and unlocking opportunities for learners of all backgrounds. By embracing technology in education, we can empower individuals, transform communities, and shape a brighter future for Zambia."

The students left the hall, their minds buzzing with new-found insights into the potential of technology to revolutionize education in Zambia. They understood that by embracing innovation and digital transformation, they could pave the way for a more equitable and accessible education system for all.

Dr. Mwansa watched them go, filled with hope for the impact they would make as future leaders and innovators in Zambia's journey towards educational excellence. He knew that with their passion, determination, and commitment to leveraging technology for learning, they would continue to drive progress and positive change, shaping a future where every Zambian has the opportunity to receive a quality education, regardless of their circumstances.

Educational Policy and Reform in Zambia

The lecture hall brimmed with anticipation as Dr. Mwansa prepared to unravel the complexities of educational policy and reform in Zambia. The students, their faces a blend of curiosity and determination, leaned forward in their seats, eager to understand how policy decisions could shape the future of education in their country.

"Good afternoon, everyone," Dr. Mwansa greeted, his voice resonating with authority and conviction. "Today, we embark on a journey through the realm of educational policy and reform in Zambia, a journey that holds the key to unlocking the potential of our education system and shaping the trajectory of our nation's future."

With a click, the screen illuminated, revealing images

of policymakers, educators, and stakeholders engaged in discussions and debates about education reform. "Educational policy serves as the roadmap for our education system, guiding decision-making, setting priorities, and allocating resources," Dr. Mwansa began. "In Zambia, as in many countries, educational policy plays a crucial role in addressing the challenges facing our education system and ensuring that every learner has access to a quality education."

The next slide displayed diagrams illustrating the various components of educational policy, from curriculum development to teacher training and school governance. "Zambia faces significant challenges in formulating and implementing effective educational policies," Dr. Mwansa continued. "Issues such as limited funding, political instability, and competing priorities often hinder efforts to enact meaningful reforms and address the root causes of educational inequality and underachievement."

A student raised her hand. "How can we overcome these challenges and enact meaningful educational reforms in Zambia?"

"An excellent question," Dr. Mwansa replied, bringing up a slide highlighting strategies for educational policy and reform. "Enacting meaningful educational reforms requires a collaborative and evidence-based approach that engages all stakeholders, from policymakers and educators to parents and communities."

He then displayed images of policy forums, stakeholder consultations, and policy research initiatives. "It begins with conducting a thorough assessment of the strengths and weaknesses of our education system and identifying key areas for improvement," Dr. Mwansa explained. "It also involves setting clear goals and targets, developing comprehensive policies and strategies, and allocating adequate resources to support implementation and monitoring."

A student in the front row raised his hand. "How can we ensure that educational policies are responsive to the needs and aspirations of Zambian learners?"

"Educational policies must be grounded in the realities of our learners' lives and experiences, taking into account their diverse backgrounds, interests, and aspirations," Dr. Mwansa replied, transitioning to a slide showing examples of learner-centered policies. "This requires meaningful engagement with learners, parents, and communities throughout the policy development process, as well as ongoing feedback and evaluation to ensure that policies are responsive to changing needs and priorities."

He then displayed graphs showing the positive impact of evidence-based policy reforms on various educational indicators, from student achievement to school retention rates. "Moreover, educational policy should be guided by principles of equity, inclusion, and social justice, ensuring that every learner has access to a quality education, regardless of their background or circumstances," Dr. Mwansa concluded. "By working together to enact meaningful educational reforms, we can build a more equitable, inclusive, and high-performing education system for Zambia."

As the lecture concluded, Dr. Mwansa left the students with a final thought. "Educational policy is not just a set of rules and regulations; it is a reflection of our values, aspirations, and commitment to the future of our nation. By engaging in the policy process, advocating for change, and holding policymakers accountable, we can shape the direction of education in Zambia and unlock opportunities for all learners to thrive."

The students left the hall, their minds buzzing with new-found insights into the importance of educational policy and reform in shaping the future of their country. They understood that by engaging in the policy process and advocating for change, they could contribute to a more equitable, inclusive, and high-performing education system for Zambia.

Dr. Mwansa watched them go, filled with hope for the impact they would make as future leaders and advocates for educational reform. He knew that with their passion, determination, and commitment to excellence, they would continue to drive progress and positive change, shaping a future where every Zambian has the opportunity to receive a quality education and fulfill their potential.

10

Chapter 10: Gender and Development

Gender Theories and Frameworks Applied in Zambia

The lecture hall filled with a palpable sense of anticipation as Dr. Mwansa prepared to delve into the intricate realm of gender and development in Zambia. The students, their faces a mix of curiosity and determination, eagerly awaited insights into the complex interplay between gender dynamics and societal progress.

"Good afternoon, everyone," Dr. Mwansa greeted, his voice carrying a tone of authority and empathy. "Today, we embark on a journey through the realm of gender and development in Zambia, exploring the theories and frameworks that shape our understanding of gender dynamics and their implications for societal advancement."

With a click, the screen illuminated, revealing images of men and women engaged in various aspects of daily life, from work and education to family and community roles. "Gender is more than just a biological distinction;

it is a social construct that influences our identities, roles, and opportunities in society," Dr. Mwansa began. "In Zambia, as in many countries, gender dynamics intersect with other dimensions of inequality, such as class, ethnicity, and geography, shaping the experiences and opportunities of individuals and communities."

The next slide displayed diagrams illustrating the various theories and frameworks used to analyze gender dynamics, from feminist theory to intersectionality and masculinity studies. "Zambia faces significant challenges in addressing gender inequality and promoting gender equality," Dr. Mwansa continued. "Issues such as unequal access to education and employment, gender-based violence, and discriminatory social norms often perpetuate inequalities and limit the full participation and contribution of women and girls in society."

A student raised her hand. "How can we apply gender theories and frameworks to address gender inequality in Zambia?"

"An excellent question," Dr. Mwansa replied, bringing up a slide highlighting strategies for applying gender theories and frameworks. "Applying gender theories and frameworks requires a multi-faceted approach that addresses the root causes of gender inequality and promotes transformative change at individual, community, and societal levels."

He then displayed images of gender-sensitive policies, gender mainstreaming initiatives, and community empowerment programs. "It begins with raising awareness about gender issues and challenging harmful stereotypes and norms that perpetuate inequality and discrimination," Dr. Mwansa explained. "It also involves promoting women's leadership and participation in decision-making processes, ensuring equal access to education, healthcare, and economic opportunities, and addressing the structural barriers that limit women's autonomy and agency."

A student in the front row raised her hand. "How can we engage men and boys as allies in promoting gender equality in Zambia?"

"Engaging men and boys is essential for promoting gender equality and challenging traditional notions of masculinity that perpetuate harmful gender norms and behaviors," Dr. Mwansa replied, transitioning to a slide showing examples of initiatives to engage men and boys in gender equality efforts. "This includes promoting positive masculinity, fostering healthy relationships and communication skills, and creating safe spaces for men and boys to discuss and challenge harmful gender stereotypes and attitudes."

He then displayed graphs showing the positive impact of gender-sensitive interventions on various indicators, from women's empowerment to community development. "Moreover, promoting gender equality is not just a matter of social justice; it is also essential for achieving sustainable development and inclusive growth," Dr. Mwansa concluded. "By working together to apply gender theories and frameworks, we can build a more equitable, inclusive, and prosperous society for Zambia."

As the lecture concluded, Dr. Mwansa left the students with a final thought. "Gender equality is not just a women's issue; it is a human rights issue that affects us all. By embracing gender equality as a fundamental principle and working together to challenge gender stereotypes and promote equal opportunities for all, we can build a future where every Zambian, regardless of gender, has the opportunity to thrive."

The students left the hall, their minds buzzing with new-found insights into the complexities of gender dynamics and the importance of promoting gender equality in Zambia. They understood that by applying gender theories and frameworks, challenging stereotypes, and advocating for change, they could contribute to a more just, inclusive, and equitable society for all.

Dr. Mwansa watched them go, filled with hope for the impact they would make as future leaders and change-makers in Zambia's journey towards gender equality. He knew that with their passion, determination, and commitment to social justice, they would continue to drive progress and positive change, shaping a future where every Zambian, regardless of gender, has the opportunity to realize their full potential.

Gender Mainstreaming in Zambian Policies

The atmosphere in the lecture hall brimmed with anticipation as Dr. Mwansa delved deeper into the intricate topic of gender mainstreaming in Zambian policies. The students, their eyes alight with curiosity and determination, leaned forward in their seats, eager to grasp the nuances of integrating gender perspectives into policy frameworks.

"Good afternoon, everyone," Dr. Mwansa greeted, his voice carrying a blend of authority and empathy. "Today, we continue our exploration of gender and development in Zambia by examining the critical concept of gender mainstreaming in policymaking."

With a click, the screen illuminated, revealing images of policymakers, activists, and community leaders engaged in discussions and debates about gender equality and women's empowerment. "Gender mainstreaming is a strategy for integrating gender perspectives into all stages of policymaking, implementation, and evaluation," Dr. Mwansa began. "In Zambia, as in many countries, gender mainstreaming is a key tool for promoting gender equality and ensuring that policies and programs address the specific needs and priorities of women and men."

The next slide displayed diagrams illustrating the various components of gender mainstreaming, from gender analysis to gender-responsive budgeting and monitoring. "Zambia faces significant challenges in mainstreaming gender into policymaking processes," Dr. Mwansa continued. "Issues such as limited capacity, inadequate resources, and resistance to change often hinder efforts to institutionalize gender equality and ensure that policies are responsive to the diverse needs and experiences of women and men."

A student raised her hand. "How can we overcome these challenges and promote gender mainstreaming in Zambian policies?"

"An excellent question," Dr. Mwansa replied, bringing up a slide highlighting strategies for promoting gender mainstreaming. "Promoting gender mainstreaming requires a multi-faceted approach that addresses both the technical and political dimensions of policymaking."

He then displayed images of gender training workshops, gender analysis tools, and gender-sensitive policy guidelines. "It begins with building the capacity of policymakers and other stakeholders to understand and apply gender analysis tools and methodologies," Dr. Mwansa explained. "It also involves creating incentives and accountability mechanisms to ensure that gender considerations are integrated into all stages of the policy making process, from agenda setting to implementation and monitoring."

A student in the front row raised her hand. "How can we ensure that gender mainstreaming leads to meaningful changes in the lives of women and men in Zambia?"

"Gender mainstreaming must go beyond tokenism and rhetoric to create real, tangible changes in the lives of women and men," Dr. Mwansa replied, transitioning to a slide showing examples of gender mainstreaming initiatives. "This requires actively involving women and men in the policy making process, ensuring their meaningful participation and representation, and addressing the structural barriers that perpetuate gender inequality and discrimination."

He then displayed graphs showing the positive impact of gender mainstreaming on various indicators, from women's economic empowerment to gender-based violence prevention. "Moreover, gender mainstreaming is not just a technical exercise; it is a political commitment to advancing gender equality and women's rights," Dr. Mwansa concluded. "By working together to promote gender mainstreaming in Zambian policies, we can build a more inclusive, equitable, and just society for all."

As the lecture concluded, Dr. Mwansa left the students with a final thought. "Gender mainstreaming is not just about ticking boxes or meeting quotas; it is about transforming systems and structures to ensure that the rights and needs of women and men are equally valued and addressed. By embracing gender mainstreaming as a guiding principle and advocating for change, we can build a future where every Zambian, regardless of gender, has the opportunity to thrive."

The students left the hall, their minds buzzing with new-found insights into the importance of gender mainstreaming in policymaking and its potential to drive meaningful change in Zambia. They understood that by promoting gender mainstreaming, challenging gender norms, and advocating for gender equality, they could contribute to a more just, inclusive, and equitable society for all.

Dr. Mwansa watched them go, filled with hope for the impact they would make as future leaders and advocates for gender equality in Zambia. He knew that with their passion, determination, and commitment to social justice, they would continue to drive progress and positive change, shaping a future where every Zambian, regardless of gender, has the opportunity to realize their full potential.

Women's Rights and Empowerment in Zambia

The lecture hall was charged with anticipation as Dr. Mwansa delved into the profound topic of women's rights and empowerment in Zambia. The students, their faces illuminated with a blend of empathy and determination, leaned forward in their seats, eager to understand the complexities of gender equality and women's empowerment.

"Good afternoon, everyone," Dr. Mwansa greeted, his voice resonating with passion and conviction. "Today, we continue our exploration of gender and development in Zambia by delving into the critical issue of women's rights and empowerment."

With a click, the screen came to life, displaying images of women from diverse backgrounds, engaged in various spheres of life, from politics and business to education and activism. "Women's rights are human rights," Dr. Mwansa began, his voice carrying the weight of centuries of struggle and resilience. "In Zambia, as in many parts of the world, women continue to face systemic discrimination and marginalization, depriving them of their fundamental rights and opportunities."

The next slide showcased statistics highlighting the gender disparities in Zambia, from educational attainment to political representation and economic participation. "Zambia faces significant challenges in advancing women's rights and empowerment," Dr. Mwansa continued. "Issues such as gender-based violence, limited access to education and healthcare, and discriminatory laws and customs often perpetuate inequalities and limit women's ability to fully participate in society."

A student raised her hand. "How can we overcome these challenges and empower women in Zambia?"

"An excellent question," Dr. Mwansa replied, bringing up a slide highlighting strategies for promoting women's rights and empowerment. "Empowering women requires a multi-faceted approach that addresses the root causes of gender inequality and discrimination."

He then displayed images of women's empowerment programs, legal reform initiatives, and grassroots movements. "It begins with enacting and enforcing laws and policies that protect and promote women's rights, including laws against gender-based violence and discrimination," Dr. Mwansa explained. "It also involves providing women with access to education, healthcare, and economic opportunities, as well as creating enabling environments for women's participation in decision-making and leadership roles."

A student in the front row raised her hand. "How can we engage men and boys as allies in promoting women's rights and empowerment?"

"Engaging men and boys is essential for promoting gender equality and challenging harmful gender norms and behaviors," Dr. Mwansa replied, transitioning to a slide showing examples of initiatives to engage men and boys in women's empowerment efforts. "This includes promoting positive masculinity, fostering empathy and respect for women's rights, and creating safe spaces for men and boys to confront and address issues of gender-based violence and discrimination."

He then displayed graphs showing the positive impact of women's empowerment on various indicators, from economic growth to social cohesion and stability. "Moreover, empowering women is not just a matter of social justice; it is also essential for achieving sustainable development and inclusive growth," Dr. Mwansa concluded. "By working together to promote women's rights and empowerment in Zambia, we can build a more equitable, inclusive, and prosperous society for all."

As the lecture concluded, Dr. Mwansa left the students with a final thought. "Women's rights are not negotiable; they are non-negotiable. By embracing women's rights and empowerment as fundamental principles and advocating for change, we can build a future where every Zambian, regardless of gender, has the opportunity to thrive."

The students left the hall, their hearts stirred with newfound determination to champion women's rights and empowerment in Zambia. They understood that by promoting gender equality, challenging gender norms, and advocating for women's rights, they could contribute to a more just, inclusive, and equitable society for all.

Dr. Mwansa watched them go, filled with hope for the

impact they would make as future leaders and change-makers in Zambia's journey towards gender equality. He knew that with their passion, determination, and commitment to social justice, they would continue to drive progress and positive change, shaping a future where every Zambian, regardless of gender, has the opportunity to realize their full potential.

Gender-Based Violence in Zambia

The atmosphere in the lecture hall turned somber as Dr. Mwansa broached the sensitive and urgent topic of gender-based violence (GBV) in Zambia. The students, their expressions a mix of concern and determination, leaned in attentively, ready to confront the harsh realities that many Zambians, particularly women and girls, face.

"Good afternoon, everyone," Dr. Mwansa began, his voice now filled with empathy and resolve. "Today, we confront a grave challenge that plagues our society: gender-based violence."

With a click, the screen displayed distressing statistics and images of survivors, illustrating the harsh realities of GBV in Zambia. "Gender-based violence, in all its forms, is a violation of human rights and a grave injustice," Dr. Mwansa stated firmly. "In Zambia, as in many parts of the world, women and girls bear the brunt of this violence, suffering physical, emotional, and psychological harm at the hands of perpetrators who seek to exert power and control."

The next slide showed data on the prevalence of GBV in Zambia, from intimate partner violence to sexual assault and femicide. "Zambia faces significant challenges in addressing gender-based violence," Dr. Mwansa continued.

"Deep-rooted social norms, cultural beliefs, and economic inequalities often perpetuate a culture of impunity and silence, making it difficult for survivors to seek help and justice."

A student raised her hand, her voice trembling with concern. "What can we do to combat gender-based violence in Zambia?"

Dr. Mwansa nodded, acknowledging the urgency of the question. "Combating gender-based violence requires a comprehensive and coordinated response from all sectors of society," he explained, bringing up a slide outlining strategies for addressing GBV. "It begins with raising awareness about the issue and challenging the attitudes and beliefs that condone violence against women and girls."

He then displayed images of GBV prevention campaigns, support services for survivors, and legal reforms aimed at strengthening protections and accountability. "It also involves providing survivors with access to comprehensive support services, including medical care, counseling, and legal assistance," Dr. Mwansa continued. "And it requires holding perpetrators accountable for their actions through robust law enforcement and judicial systems that prioritize the rights and safety of survivors."

A student in the front row spoke up, her voice resolute. "How can we break the cycle of violence and create a society where all Zambians can live free from fear?"

Dr. Mwansa nodded, recognizing the importance of breaking the cycle of violence. "Breaking the cycle of violence requires a collective effort to challenge the root causes of GBV and promote gender equality and respect for human rights," he replied, transitioning to a slide showing examples of community-based initiatives to prevent GBV.

"This includes promoting healthy and equitable relationships, empowering women and girls to assert their rights and access opportunities, and engaging men and boys as allies in challenging harmful gender norms and behaviors," Dr. Mwansa explained. "It also involves creating safe and supportive environments where survivors can seek help and support without fear of stigma or retaliation."

He then displayed graphs showing the positive impact of GBV prevention programs on various indicators, from survivor empowerment to community cohesion and safety. "Moreover, preventing gender-based violence is not just a moral imperative; it is also essential for achieving sustainable development and inclusive growth," Dr. Mwansa concluded. "By working together to combat gender-based violence in Zambia, we can build a future where every Zambian, regardless of gender, can live free from fear and violence."

As the lecture concluded, Dr. Mwansa left the students with a final thought. "Gender-based violence is not inevitable; it is preventable. By standing together, speaking out, and taking action, we can create a Zambia where every individual is treated with dignity, respect, and equality."

The students left the hall, their hearts heavy with the weight of the challenge ahead, but also filled with a renewed sense of determination to combat gender-based violence in Zambia. They understood that by raising awareness, providing support, and advocating for change, they could contribute to a society where all individuals, regardless of gender, can live free from fear and violence.

Dr. Mwansa watched them go, filled with hope for the impact they would make as future leaders and change-makers in Zambia's journey towards ending gender-based violence. He knew that with their passion, determination, and commitment to social justice, they would continue to drive progress and positive change, shaping a future where every Zambian can live a life of dignity, equality, and safety.

Gender and Economic Development in Zambia

The lecture hall buzzed with anticipation as Dr. Mwansa delved into the crucial intersection of gender and economic development in Zambia. The students, their eyes bright with curiosity and determination, leaned forward in their seats, eager to explore how gender dynamics shape economic opportunities and outcomes.

"Good afternoon, everyone," Dr. Mwansa greeted, his voice resonating with authority and empathy. "Today, we continue our journey through gender and development in Zambia by examining the critical link between gender and economic development."

With a click, the screen illuminated, displaying images of women and men engaged in various economic activities, from farming and entrepreneurship to formal employment and informal labor. "Gender plays a significant role in shaping economic opportunities and outcomes in Zambia," Dr. Mwansa began. "Despite progress in recent years, women continue to face systemic barriers that limit their access to resources, markets, and decision-making power."

The next slide showcased statistics highlighting the gender gaps in economic participation and outcomes, from labor force participation rates to earnings and access to finance. "Zambia faces significant challenges in promoting gender equality in the economy," Dr. Mwansa continued. "Issues such as limited access to land and property rights, unequal pay for equal work, and discriminatory social norms often perpetuate inequalities and hinder women's ability to fully participate in and benefit from economic development."

A student raised her hand, her voice filled with concern. "How can we address these challenges and promote gender equality in Zambia's economy?"

"An excellent question," Dr. Mwansa replied, bringing up a slide outlining strategies for promoting gender equality in the economy. "Promoting gender equality in the economy requires a multi-faceted approach that addresses both the structural and cultural barriers that limit women's economic opportunities."

He then displayed images of initiatives to promote women's entrepreneurship, improve access to finance and market opportunities, and strengthen women's land and property rights. "It begins with creating an enabling environment that supports women's economic empowerment, including policies and programs that promote equal access to education, training, and employment opportunities," Dr. Mwansa explained. "It also involves addressing the root causes of gender inequality, such as discriminatory social norms and practices that limit women's autonomy and agency."

A student in the front row spoke up, her voice filled with determination. "How can we ensure that women's economic empowerment leads to sustainable and inclusive growth in Zambia?"

Dr. Mwansa nodded, acknowledging the importance of sustainable and inclusive growth. "Ensuring that women's economic empowerment leads to sustainable and inclusive growth requires a holistic approach that integrates gender considerations into all stages of the development process," he replied, transitioning to a slide showing examples of gender-responsive economic development initiatives.

"This includes promoting women's participation in decision-making and leadership roles, investing in gender-responsive infrastructure and services, and fostering an enabling business environment that supports women entrepreneurs and small businesses," Dr. Mwansa explained. "It also involves addressing the gender gaps in access to finance, technology, and markets, and promoting women's representation and leadership in key economic sectors."

He then displayed graphs showing the positive impact of women's economic empowerment on various indicators, from poverty reduction to economic growth and social cohesion. "Moreover, promoting gender equality in the economy is not just a matter of social justice; it is also essential for achieving sustainable development and inclusive growth," Dr. Mwansa concluded. "By working together to promote women's economic empowerment in Zambia, we can build a future where every Zambian, regardless of gender, has the opportunity to thrive."

As the lecture concluded, Dr. Mwansa left the students with a final thought. "Women's economic empowerment is not just about increasing productivity or GDP; it is about creating a more equitable, inclusive, and just society for all. By embracing women's economic empowerment as a guiding principle and advocating for change, we can build a future where every Zambian can realize their full potential."

The students left the hall, their minds buzzing with new-found insights into the importance of promoting gender equality in the economy and its potential to drive sustainable and inclusive growth in Zambia. They understood that by advocating for change, challenging gender norms, and supporting women's economic empowerment, they could contribute to a more just, inclusive, and prosperous society for all.

Dr. Mwansa watched them go, filled with hope for the impact they would make as future leaders and change-makers in Zambia's journey towards gender equality. He knew that with their passion, determination, and commitment to social justice, they would continue to drive progress and positive change, shaping a future where every Zambian, regardless of gender, has the opportunity to thrive.

Policy and Legal Reforms for Gender Equality in Zambia

The atmosphere in the lecture hall crackled with anticipation as Dr. Mwansa embarked on the critical discussion of policy and legal reforms for gender equality in Zambia. The students, their faces alight with determination and curiosity, leaned in attentively, eager to understand the mechanisms through which laws and policies can drive transformative change.

"Good afternoon, everyone," Dr. Mwansa greeted, his voice a blend of authority and empathy. "Today, we delve into the vital realm of policy and legal reforms for gender equality in Zambia."

With a click, the screen illuminated, displaying images of legislative sessions, advocacy campaigns, and community mobilizations for gender equality. "Policy and legal frameworks are essential tools for advancing gender equality and women's rights," Dr. Mwansa began. "In Zambia, as in many countries, laws and policies shape the opportunities and outcomes for women and men, influencing everything from education and employment to healthcare and political participation."

The next slide showcased examples of gender-responsive policies and legal reforms, from laws prohibiting gender-based violence to initiatives promoting women's representation in decision-making. "Zambia has made significant strides in enacting laws and policies that promote gender equality," Dr. Mwansa continued. "However, gaps and challenges persist, requiring ongoing efforts to strengthen and implement existing frameworks and enact new ones where needed."

A student raised her hand, her voice tinged with urgency. "What are some key areas where policy and legal reforms are needed to advance gender equality in Zambia?"

"An excellent question," Dr. Mwansa replied, bringing up a slide outlining priority areas for policy and legal reforms. "Advancing gender equality requires a comprehensive and multi-sectoral approach that addresses the root causes of gender inequality and discrimination."

He then displayed images of legislative proposals and advocacy campaigns focused on issues such as gender-based violence, women's economic empowerment, and gender-responsive budgeting. "Key areas for policy and legal reforms include strengthening laws and enforcement mechanisms to address gender-based violence, promoting women's economic empowerment through measures such as equal pay and access to finance, and ensuring gender-responsive budgeting and planning processes that prioritize investments in gender equality and women's empowerment," Dr. Mwansa explained.

A student in the front row spoke up, her voice filled with determination. "How can we advocate for policy and legal reforms to advance gender equality in Zambia?"

Dr. Mwansa nodded, acknowledging the importance of advocacy and activism. "Advocating for policy and legal reforms requires collective action and strategic engagement with policymakers, legislators, civil society organizations, and other stakeholders," he replied, transitioning to a slide showing examples of advocacy strategies and coalitions for gender equality.

"This includes raising awareness about the importance of gender equality, mobilizing support for specific policy proposals, and holding decision-makers accountable for their commitments to gender equality," Dr. Mwansa explained. "It also involves building alliances and partnerships across sectors and advocating for changes in laws, policies, and practices that perpetuate gender inequality and discrimination."

He then displayed graphs showing the positive impact of policy and legal reforms on various indicators, from women's representation in leadership to access to justice and economic opportunities. "Moreover, policy and legal reforms for gender equality are not just about compliance with international standards or meeting targets; they are about creating a more just, equitable, and inclusive society for all," Dr. Mwansa concluded. "By working together to advocate for policy and legal reforms in Zambia, we can build a future where every Zambian, regardless of gender, has the opportunity to live a life of dignity, equality, and empowerment."

As the lecture concluded, Dr. Mwansa left the students with a final thought. "Policy and legal reforms are not ends in themselves; they are means to an end. By advocating for change, challenging gender norms, and supporting policy and legal reforms for gender equality, we can build a future where every Zambian can realize their full potential and contribute to the prosperity and well-being of the nation."

The students left the hall, their hearts stirred with newfound determination to advocate for policy and legal reforms that advance gender equality in Zambia. They understood that by raising their voices, mobilizing support, and holding decision-makers accountable, they could contribute to a more just, equitable, and inclusive society for all.

Dr. Mwansa watched them go, filled with hope for the impact they would make as future leaders and change-makers in Zambia's journey towards gender equality. He knew that with their passion, determination, and commitment to social justice, they would continue to drive progress and positive change, shaping a future where every Zambian, regardless of gender, has the opportunity to thrive.

11

Chapter 11: Rural Development

Rural vs. Urban Development Dynamics in Zambia

The rustling of leaves and the distant chirping of birds provided a tranquil backdrop as Dr. Mwansa delved into the complexities of rural development in Zambia. The students, their faces illuminated by the soft glow of the projector, listened intently, eager to unravel the intricate dynamics between rural and urban development.

"Good afternoon, everyone," Dr. Mwansa greeted, his voice carrying a sense of reverence for the topic at hand. "Today, we embark on a journey through the rural landscapes of Zambia and explore the dynamic interplay between rural and urban development."

With a click, the screen came to life, displaying images contrasting the bustling streets of urban centers with the serene tranquility of rural villages. "Rural development in Zambia is intricately linked to urban development, with each influencing and shaping the other in profound ways," Dr.

Mwansa began. "While urban areas often serve as centers of economic activity and innovation, rural communities are the backbone of the nation, providing food, resources, and cultural heritage."

The next slide showcased statistics highlighting the disparities between rural and urban areas in Zambia, from access to basic services to income levels and infrastructure. "Zambia faces significant challenges in promoting rural development and bridging the gap between rural and urban areas," Dr. Mwansa continued. "Historical legacies, geographical disparities, and unequal distribution of resources often exacerbate inequalities and hinder the progress of rural communities."

A student raised her hand, her voice filled with curiosity. "How do rural and urban development dynamics intersect, and what are the implications for Zambia's development?"

"An excellent question," Dr. Mwansa replied, bringing up a slide illustrating the interconnected nature of rural and urban development. "Rural and urban areas are not isolated entities but are deeply interconnected, with flows of people, goods, and resources shaping the social, economic, and environmental landscapes of both."

He then displayed images of initiatives aimed at promoting rural-urban linkages, from agricultural value chains and market integration to infrastructure development and migration patterns. "The interactions between rural and urban areas present both opportunities and challenges for Zambia's development," Dr. Mwansa explained. "On one hand, rural areas contribute to urban growth through migration, remittances, and the supply of goods and labor. On the other hand, urban areas provide markets, services, and employment opportunities that can support rural development and poverty reduction."

A student in the front row spoke up, her voice tinged with concern. "How can we ensure that rural development initiatives are inclusive and sustainable, benefiting all members of society?"

Dr. Mwansa nodded, acknowledging the importance of inclusivity and sustainability in rural development. "Ensuring that rural development initiatives are inclusive and sustainable requires a multi-dimensional approach that addresses the diverse needs and aspirations of rural communities," he replied, transitioning to a slide showing examples of inclusive rural development strategies.

"This includes promoting participatory approaches to decision-making, strengthening local governance structures, and empowering marginalized groups, such as women and youth, to actively participate in and benefit from development processes," Dr. Mwansa explained. "It also involves investing in basic services, infrastructure, and social protection programs that improve livelihoods, reduce vulnerabilities, and enhance resilience to shocks and stresses."

He then displayed graphs showing the positive impact of inclusive rural development on various indicators, from poverty reduction to social cohesion and environmental sustainability. "Moreover, promoting rural development is not just about improving living standards or economic growth; it is about building resilient, thriving, and inclusive communities that can withstand and adapt to change," Dr. Mwansa concluded. "By working together to promote rural development in Zambia, we can build a future where every Zambian, regardless of location, has the opportunity to thrive and prosper."

As the lecture concluded, Dr. Mwansa left the students with a final thought. "Rural development is not a destination; it is a journey. By embracing the interconnectedness of rural and urban areas and advocating for inclusive and sustainable development approaches, we can build a future where every Zambian community can flourish and contribute to the prosperity and well-being of the nation."

The students left the hall, their minds buzzing with new-found insights into the complexities of rural development and its implications for Zambia's journey towards prosperity. They understood that by embracing inclusivity, sustainability, and resilience, they could contribute to building a future where every Zambian, whether in rural or urban areas, has the opportunity to thrive.

Dr. Mwansa watched them go, filled with hope for the im-pact they would make as future leaders and change-makers in Zambia's rural development. He knew that with their passion, determination, and commitment to social justice, they would continue to drive progress and positive change, shaping a future where every Zambian community can flourish and prosper.

Agricultural Development in Zambian Villages

The serene ambiance of the lecture hall shifted to a vibrant depiction of Zambian village life as Dr. Mwansa delved into the intricacies of agricultural development. The students, cap-tivated by the imagery of lush fields and bustling marketplaces, leaned forward in anticipation, eager to explore the vital role of agriculture in rural communities.

"Good afternoon, everyone," Dr. Mwansa greeted, his

voice resonating with warmth and expertise. "Today, we venture into the heart of Zambian villages and uncover the transformative power of agricultural development."

With a click, the screen illuminated, showcasing images of farmers tilling the land, tending to livestock, and harvesting bountiful crops. "Agriculture is the lifeblood of Zambian villages, providing sustenance, livelihoods, and cultural heritage to rural communities," Dr. Mwansa began. "From smallholder farmers to agro-processors and market vendors, agriculture encompasses a wide spectrum of activities that drive economic growth and social development in rural areas."

The next slide displayed statistics highlighting the significance of agriculture in Zambia's economy, from its contribution to GDP to its role in employment and food security. "Zambia's agricultural sector holds immense potential for unlocking rural prosperity and reducing poverty," Dr. Mwansa continued. "However, it also faces numerous challenges, including limited access to markets, inputs, and finance, as well as vulnerability to climate change and environmental degradation."

A student raised her hand, her voice brimming with curiosity. "How can agricultural development initiatives empower rural communities and foster sustainable livelihoods?"

"An excellent question," Dr. Mwansa replied, bringing up a slide illustrating strategies for promoting agricultural development in Zambian villages. "Empowering rural communities and fostering sustainable livelihoods requires a holistic approach that addresses the multifaceted dimensions of agricultural development."

He then displayed images of initiatives aimed at enhancing productivity, improving market access, and promoting sustainable farming practices. "Key interventions include investing in agricultural extension services, providing access to inputs and technologies, strengthening market linkages, and promoting climate-smart agriculture," Dr. Mwansa explained. "It also involves empowering smallholder farmers, particularly women and youth, to diversify their livelihoods, build resilience to shocks, and participate in value chains."

A student in the front row spoke up, her voice filled with determination. "How can we ensure that agricultural development initiatives are inclusive and benefit all members of rural communities?"

Dr. Mwansa nodded, acknowledging the importance of inclusivity in agricultural development. "Ensuring that agricultural development initiatives are inclusive requires addressing the diverse needs and priorities of rural communities," he replied, transitioning to a slide showing examples of inclusive agricultural development approaches.

"This includes promoting gender-responsive agriculture, ensuring equitable access to resources and opportunities, and empowering marginalized groups, such as women and youth, to actively participate in decision-making and value chains," Dr. Mwansa explained. "It also involves promoting sustainable land management practices, enhancing access to finance and social protection, and fostering partnerships and collaboration among stakeholders."

He then displayed graphs showing the positive impact of inclusive agricultural development on various indicators, from poverty reduction to food security and environmental sustainability. "Moreover, promoting agricultural development is not just about increasing productivity or incomes; it is about building resilient, thriving, and inclusive rural communities that can withstand and adapt to change," Dr. Mwansa concluded. "By working together to promote agricultural development in Zambian villages, we can build a future where every rural community can flourish and prosper."

As the lecture concluded, Dr. Mwansa left the students with a final thought. "Agricultural development is not a solitary endeavor; it is a collective effort. By embracing inclusivity, sustainability, and resilience, we can unlock the full potential of Zambia's agricultural sector and create a brighter future for rural communities across the nation."

The students left the hall, their minds buzzing with new-found insights into the transformative power of agriculture in rural development. They understood that by championing inclusive and sustainable agricultural initiatives, they could contribute to building resilient and prosperous rural communities in Zambia.

Dr. Mwansa watched them go, filled with hope for the impact they would make as future leaders and change-makers in Zambia's agricultural development. He knew that with their passion, determination, and commitment to rural prosperity, they would continue to drive progress and positive change, shaping a future where every Zambian village can thrive and prosper.

Rural Infrastructure and Services in Zambia

The ambiance in the lecture hall transitioned to a vivid portrayal of rural landscapes as Dr. Mwansa delved into the importance of infrastructure and services in Zambia's villages. The students, captivated by the imagery of dirt roads winding through verdant fields and simple yet bustling marketplaces, leaned forward in anticipation, eager to explore the vital role of rural infrastructure and services.

"Good afternoon, everyone," Dr. Mwansa greeted, his voice resonating with warmth and expertise. "Today, we venture into the heart of Zambia's rural communities and uncover the significance of infrastructure and services in shaping their development."

With a click, the screen illuminated, showcasing images of village paths, bridges spanning gentle streams, and community centers buzzing with activity. "Infrastructure and services are the backbone of rural development, providing essential linkages, connectivity, and support to communities," Dr. Mwansa began. "From transportation and communication networks to healthcare facilities and educational institutions, rural infrastructure and services play a critical role in improving livelihoods, enhancing access to opportunities, and promoting social cohesion."

The next slide displayed statistics highlighting the challenges faced by rural communities in accessing basic infrastructure and services, from inadequate road networks to limited healthcare facilities and educational resources. "Zambia's rural areas often lag behind urban centers in terms of infrastructure and service provision, leading to disparities in access and opportunities," Dr. Mwansa continued. "Addressing these challenges requires concerted efforts to invest in and prioritize rural infrastructure and services."

A student raised her hand, her voice filled with curiosity. "How can rural infrastructure and services be improved to better meet the needs of communities?"

"An excellent question," Dr. Mwansa replied, bringing up a slide illustrating strategies for enhancing rural infrastructure and services in Zambia. "Improving rural infrastructure and services requires a multi-dimensional approach that addresses the diverse needs and priorities of communities."

He then displayed images of initiatives aimed at upgrading road networks, expanding access to clean water and sanitation, and strengthening healthcare and educational systems. "Key interventions include investing in rural road construction and maintenance, upgrading water supply and sanitation facilities, and expanding access to quality healthcare and education," Dr. Mwansa explained. "It also involves promoting renewable energy sources, enhancing digital connectivity, and fostering community participation in decision-making and service delivery."

A student in the front row spoke up, her voice brimming with determination. "How can we ensure that rural infrastructure and services are sustainable and resilient to environmental and socio-economic changes?"

Dr. Mwansa nodded, acknowledging the importance of sustainability and resilience in rural development. "Ensuring that rural infrastructure and services are sustainable requires integrating environmental considerations, promoting resource efficiency, and building resilience to climate change and other shocks," he replied, transitioning to a slide showing examples of sustainable rural development approaches.

"This includes adopting green infrastructure solutions, such as nature-based drainage systems and renewable energy technologies, and incorporating climate-smart practices into infrastructure design and management," Dr. Mwansa explained. "It also involves building local capacities, strengthening governance structures, and fostering partnerships and collaboration among stakeholders."

He then displayed graphs showing the positive impact of sustainable rural infrastructure and services on various indicators, from economic growth to environmental conservation and community well-being. "Moreover, promoting sustainable rural development is not just about meeting immediate needs; it is about building resilient, thriving, and inclusive communities that can adapt and thrive in the face of change," Dr. Mwansa concluded. "By working together to improve rural infrastructure and services in Zambia, we can build a future where every rural community can flourish and prosper."

As the lecture concluded, Dr. Mwansa left the students with a final thought. "Rural infrastructure and services are not just physical structures; they are pathways to progress and prosperity. By embracing sustainability, resilience, and inclusivity, we can unlock the full potential of Zambia's rural areas and create a brighter future for all."

The students left the hall, their minds buzzing with newfound insights into the critical role of infrastructure and services in rural development. They understood that by championing sustainable and resilient approaches, they could contribute to building thriving and inclusive communities in Zambia's villages.

Dr. Mwansa watched them go, filled with hope for the impact they would make as future leaders and change-makers in Zambia's rural development. He knew that with their passion, determination, and commitment to rural prosperity, they would continue to drive progress and positive change, shaping a future where every Zambian village can thrive and prosper.

Land Rights and Land Use in Zambia

The lecture hall transformed into a scene of rural landscapes as Dr. Mwansa delved into the intricate dynamics of land rights and land use in Zambia. The students, captivated by the imagery of vast fields, communal grazing lands, and traditional homesteads, listened intently, eager to explore the complexities of land tenure and its implications for rural development.

"Good afternoon, everyone," Dr. Mwansa greeted, his voice carrying a sense of reverence for the topic at hand. "Today, we journey into the heart of Zambia's rural communities and delve into the significance of land rights and land use in shaping their development."

With a click, the screen came to life, displaying images contrasting the patchwork of land ownership and land use practices across Zambia's diverse landscapes. "Land is a precious resource in Zambia, serving as the foundation of livelihoods, cultural heritage, and social cohesion," Dr. Mwansa began. "From smallholder farms and communal grazing lands to protected areas and urban settlements, land plays a critical role in shaping the fabric of rural life."

The next slide showcased statistics highlighting the complexities of land tenure in Zambia, from customary land tenure systems to statutory land laws and land registration processes. "Zambia's land tenure system is characterized by a mix of customary and statutory arrangements, each with its own norms, practices, and governance structures," Dr. Mwansa continued. "This diversity presents both opportunities and challenges for rural development, as different land tenure systems may have varying implications for land access, use, and management."

A student raised her hand, her voice tinged with curiosity. "How do land rights and land use practices impact rural development in Zambia?"

"An excellent question," Dr. Mwansa replied, bringing up a slide illustrating the complexities of land rights and land use in rural communities. "Land rights and land use practices play a central role in shaping rural livelihoods, resource management, and community dynamics."

He then displayed images of initiatives aimed at promoting secure land tenure, sustainable land management, and equitable access to land resources. "Key interventions include strengthening land governance institutions, formalizing land rights through registration and titling processes, and promoting participatory land-use planning and management," Dr. Mwansa explained. "It also involves addressing land-related conflicts and grievances, enhancing women's land rights and tenure security, and ensuring that land-use practices are environmentally sustainable and socially inclusive."

A student in the front row spoke up, her voice filled with concern. "How can we reconcile competing interests and ensure that land rights are respected and upheld in rural communities?"

Dr. Mwansa nodded, acknowledging the complexity of land tenure issues in rural areas. "Reconciling competing interests and upholding land rights requires a collaborative and inclusive approach that engages all stakeholders," he replied, transitioning to a slide showing examples of participatory land governance processes.

"This includes facilitating dialogue and negotiation among land users, traditional authorities, government agencies, and other stakeholders to identify and address land-related challenges," Dr. Mwansa explained. "It also involves promoting legal literacy and awareness among rural communities, ensuring that land laws and policies are transparent, accessible, and equitable."

He then displayed graphs showing the positive impact of secure land tenure and sustainable land use on various indicators, from poverty reduction to environmental conservation and social cohesion. "Moreover, promoting secure land rights and sustainable land use is not just about legal frameworks; it is about building trust, fostering cooperation, and empowering communities to shape their own development," Dr. Mwansa concluded. "By working together to address land tenure challenges in Zambia, we can create a future where every rural community can thrive and prosper."

As the lecture concluded, Dr. Mwansa left the students with a final thought. "Land rights and land use are not just abstract concepts; they are the foundation of rural development. By embracing inclusivity, sustainability, and resilience, we can unlock the full potential of Zambia's land resources and create a brighter future for all."

The students left the hall, their minds buzzing with new-found insights into the complexities of land tenure and its implications for rural development. They understood that by championing secure land rights and sustainable land use practices, they could contribute to building resilient and prosperous rural communities in Zambia.

Dr. Mwansa watched them go, filled with hope for the impact they would make as future leaders and change-makers in Zambia's rural development. He knew that with their passion, determination, and commitment to land rights, they would continue to drive progress and positive change, shaping a future where every Zambian village can thrive and prosper.

Rural Poverty and Inequality in Zambia

The lecture hall transformed into a depiction of rural life in Zambia as Dr. Mwansa delved into the sobering realities of poverty and inequality in the country's villages. The students, captivated by the imagery of modest homes, subsistence farming, and crowded marketplaces, listened intently, their hearts heavy with the weight of the challenges faced by rural communities.

"Good afternoon, everyone," Dr. Mwansa greeted, his voice carrying a tone of solemnity befitting the gravity of the topic. "Today, we confront the harsh realities of rural poverty and inequality in Zambia and explore the profound impact they have on the lives of millions."

With a click, the screen illuminated, displaying images contrasting the stark contrasts between wealth and destitution in Zambia's rural landscapes. "Rural poverty and inequality are pervasive and persistent challenges that undermine the well-being and prospects of millions of Zambians," Dr. Mwansa began. "From inadequate access to basic services and limited economic opportunities to social exclusion and marginalization, rural communities face a myriad of obstacles that perpetuate cycles of poverty and deprivation."

The next slide showcased statistics highlighting the extent and depth of rural poverty in Zambia, from high levels of income inequality to widespread deprivation and vulnerability. "Zambia's rural areas are disproportionately affected by poverty, with a significant portion of the population living below the poverty line and lacking access to essential services," Dr. Mwansa continued. "Moreover, rural poverty is not just an economic issue; it is also a social, political, and environmental phenomenon that intersects with other forms of inequality and marginalization."

A student raised her hand, her voice tinged with concern. "How can rural poverty be alleviated, and what role can development interventions play in addressing this issue?"

"An excellent question," Dr. Mwansa replied, bringing up a slide illustrating strategies for combating rural poverty and inequality in Zambia. "Alleviating rural poverty requires a comprehensive and multi-dimensional approach that addresses its root causes and underlying drivers."

He then displayed images of initiatives aimed at promoting inclusive economic growth, expanding access to social protection, and empowering marginalized groups. "Key interventions include promoting pro-poor agricultural and rural development strategies, enhancing access to productive resources and markets, and investing in human capital development," Dr. Mwansa explained. "It also involves strengthening social protection systems, expanding access to basic services such as education and healthcare, and fostering inclusive governance and participation."

A student in the front row spoke up, her voice filled with empathy. "How can we ensure that development interventions reach the most vulnerable and marginalized communities?"

Dr. Mwansa nodded, acknowledging the importance of targeting interventions to those most in need. "Ensuring that development interventions reach the most vulnerable and marginalized communities requires targeted and inclusive approaches that prioritize equity, participation, and empowerment," he replied, transitioning to a slide showing examples of inclusive development initiatives.

"This includes conducting comprehensive poverty assessments and vulnerability analyses to identify priority areas and target populations," Dr. Mwansa explained. "It also involves engaging communities in the design, implementation, and monitoring of development interventions, ensuring that their voices are heard and their needs are met."

He then displayed graphs showing the positive impact of inclusive development interventions on various indicators, from poverty reduction to social inclusion and community resilience. "Moreover, promoting inclusive development is not just about achieving short-term outcomes; it is about building sustainable and resilient communities that can withstand and recover from shocks," Dr. Mwansa concluded. "By working together to address rural poverty and inequality in Zambia, we can create a future where every rural community can thrive and prosper."

As the lecture concluded, Dr. Mwansa left the students with a final thought. "Rural poverty and inequality are not just statistics; they are stories of struggle, resilience, and hope. By embracing inclusivity, equity, and solidarity, we can unlock the full potential of Zambia's rural areas and create a brighter future for all."

The students left the hall, their hearts heavy with the weight of the challenges faced by rural communities, but also filled with determination to make a difference. They understood that by championing inclusive development and social justice, they could contribute to building a more equitable and prosperous Zambia.

Dr. Mwansa watched them go, filled with hope for the

impact they would make as future leaders and change-makers in Zambia's rural development. He knew that with their passion, determination, and commitment to social justice, they would continue to drive progress and positive change, shaping a future where every Zambian village can thrive and prosper.

Community Development Strategies in Rural Zambia

As the lecture hall shifted its focus to rural Zambia, Dr. Mwansa illuminated the screen with vibrant images of bustling villages and communal gatherings. The students, captivated by the scenes of community life, leaned forward in anticipation, eager to explore the strategies for community development in rural areas.

"Good afternoon, everyone," Dr. Mwansa greeted, his voice resonating with warmth and enthusiasm. "Today, we embark on a journey into the heart of rural Zambia and uncover the transformative power of community development strategies in shaping the future of our villages."

With a click, the screen came to life, displaying images of community meetings, cooperative enterprises, and grassroots initiatives. "Community development is about empowering individuals and communities to identify their needs, mobilize their resources, and take collective action to improve their lives," Dr. Mwansa began. "In rural Zambia, community development strategies play a vital role in addressing local challenges, harnessing local knowledge and resources, and building resilient and inclusive communities."

The next slide showcased statistics highlighting the impact of community development initiatives on various indicators, from poverty reduction to social cohesion and environmental sustainability. "Community development is not just about building infrastructure or delivering services; it is about fostering a sense of ownership, agency, and solidarity among community members," Dr. Mwansa continued. "It is about empowering communities to become active agents of change and partners in their own development."

A student raised her hand, her voice filled with curiosity. "What are some examples of community development strategies that have been successful in rural Zambia?"

"An excellent question," Dr. Mwansa replied, bringing up a slide illustrating examples of successful community development initiatives. "Successful community development strategies in rural Zambia encompass a range of approaches, from participatory planning and capacity building to social mobilization and collective action."

He then displayed images of initiatives aimed at promoting sustainable agriculture, enhancing access to clean water and sanitation, and strengthening local governance structures. "Key interventions include promoting community-based natural resource management, establishing community-led microfinance schemes, and supporting grassroots organizations and cooperatives," Dr. Mwansa explained. "It also involves fostering inclusive decision-making processes, strengthening social networks and solidarity, and building partnerships and collaboration among stakeholders."

A student in the front row spoke up, her voice brimming with enthusiasm. "How can we ensure that community development strategies are sustainable and responsive to the needs of rural communities?"

Dr. Mwansa nodded, acknowledging the importance of

sustainability and responsiveness in community development. "Ensuring that community development strategies are sustainable and responsive requires a participatory and adaptive approach that engages communities as partners in the development process," he replied, transitioning to a slide showing examples of sustainable community development approaches.

"This includes conducting participatory needs assessments and community consultations to identify priority areas and interventions," Dr. Mwansa explained. "It also involves building local capacities, promoting local ownership and leadership, and fostering a culture of innovation and learning."

He then displayed graphs showing the positive impact of sustainable community development strategies on various indicators, from economic growth to social inclusion and environmental resilience. "Moreover, promoting sustainable community development is not just about achieving short-term outcomes; it is about building resilient and self-reliant communities that can adapt and thrive in the face of change," Dr. Mwansa concluded. "By working together to empower communities and strengthen local capacities, we can create a future where every rural village in Zambia can flourish and prosper."

As the lecture concluded, Dr. Mwansa left the students with a final thought. "Community development is not just a process; it is a journey of empowerment, solidarity, and resilience. By embracing inclusivity, sustainability, and collaboration, we can unlock the full potential of Zambia's rural communities and build a brighter future for all."

The students left the hall, their minds buzzing with new-found insights into the transformative power of community development in rural Zambia. They understood that by championing participatory approaches and fostering local leadership, they could contribute to building vibrant and resilient communities across the country.

Dr. Mwansa watched them go, filled with hope for the impact they would make as future leaders and change-makers in Zambia's rural development. He knew that with their passion, determination, and commitment to community empowerment, they would continue to drive progress and positive change, shaping a future where every Zambian village can thrive and prosper.

12

Chapter 12: Urban Development

Urbanization Trends and Challenges in Zambia

The lecture hall transformed into a bustling cityscape as Dr. Mwansa illuminated the screen with images of urbanization in Zambia. The students, captivated by the scenes of towering skyscrapers, bustling marketplaces, and crowded streets, leaned forward in anticipation, eager to explore the trends and challenges of urban development in the country.

"Good afternoon, everyone," Dr. Mwansa greeted, his voice resonating with authority and insight. "Today, we delve into the dynamic world of urban development in Zambia and unravel the trends and challenges shaping the future of our cities."

With a click, the screen came to life, displaying statistics and graphs illustrating the rapid pace of urbanization in Zambia. "Urbanization is a defining feature of Zambia's development trajectory, with cities and towns experiencing significant population growth, economic expansion, and social transformation," Dr. Mwansa began. "From Lusaka to Ndola, from Kitwe to Livingstone, Zambia's urban centers are hubs of activity, diversity, and opportunity."

The next slide showcased statistics highlighting the scale and pace of urbanization in Zambia, from rising urban populations to expanding urban economies and infrastructures. "Urbanization brings with it a myriad of opportunities and challenges, from increased access to services and amenities to growing pressures on land, housing, and infrastructure," Dr. Mwansa continued. "It is a complex and dynamic process that requires careful planning, management, and governance."

A student raised her hand, her voice tinged with curiosity. "What are some of the key challenges associated with urbanization in Zambia?"

"An excellent question," Dr. Mwansa replied, bringing up a slide illustrating the challenges of urbanization in Zambia. "Urbanization poses a range of challenges for Zambia, from inadequate urban planning and infrastructure to social inequality and environmental degradation."

He then displayed images of congested roads, informal settlements, and pollution hotspots, highlighting the urgent need for sustainable urban development strategies. "Key challenges include managing urban growth and expansion, ensuring access to affordable housing and basic services, and addressing environmental degradation and climate change," Dr. Mwansa explained. "It also involves promoting social inclusion and equity, strengthening urban governance and management, and fostering innovation and resilience."

A student in the front row spoke up, her voice filled with concern. "How can we address these challenges and ensure that urbanization benefits all residents of Zambia?"

Dr. Mwansa nodded, acknowledging the importance of inclusive and sustainable urban development. "Addressing the challenges of urbanization requires a comprehensive and multi-sectoral approach that engages all stakeholders," he replied, transitioning to a slide showing examples of integrated urban development initiatives.

"This includes adopting sustainable urban planning and design principles, promoting mixed-use development and compact urban forms, and investing in resilient infrastructure and public services," Dr. Mwansa explained. "It also involves empowering local authorities and communities, strengthening urban governance mechanisms, and fostering partnerships and collaboration among government agencies, private sector actors, and civil society organizations."

He then displayed graphs showing the positive impact of integrated urban development initiatives on various indicators, from economic growth to social inclusion and environmental sustainability. "Moreover, promoting inclusive and sustainable urban development is not just about achieving short-term outcomes; it is about building livable, equitable, and resilient cities that can thrive and adapt in the face of change," Dr. Mwansa concluded. "By working together to address the challenges of urbanization in Zambia, we can create a future where every resident can enjoy a high quality of life and fulfill their potential."

As the lecture concluded, Dr. Mwansa left the students with a final thought. "Urbanization is not just a process; it is a journey of transformation, opportunity, and innovation. By embracing inclusivity, sustainability, and resilience, we can unlock the full potential of Zambia's cities and build a brighter

future for all."

The students left the hall, their minds buzzing with new-found insights into the complexities of urban development in Zambia. They understood that by championing inclusive and sustainable approaches, they could contribute to building vibrant, resilient, and equitable cities across the country.

Dr. Mwansa watched them go, filled with hope for the impact they would make as future leaders and change-makers in Zambia's urban development. He knew that with their passion, determination, and commitment to building better cities, they would continue to drive progress and positive change, shaping a future where every Zambian can thrive and prosper.

Housing and Slum Upgrading in Zambian Cities

The lecture hall transformed into a scene reminiscent of Zambia's bustling cities as Dr. Mwansa delved into the challenges and initiatives surrounding housing and slum upgrading. The students, immersed in the imagery of crowded neighborhoods and makeshift dwellings, leaned forward with anticipation, ready to explore the complexities of urban living in Zambia.

"Good afternoon, everyone," Dr. Mwansa greeted, his voice echoing with empathy and determination. "Today, we shine a light on the pressing issue of housing and slum upgrading in Zambia's cities, and delve into the efforts to provide dignified living conditions for all residents."

With a click, the screen illuminated with images depicting the stark contrast between modern developments and informal settlements. "Housing is a fundamental human right, yet for many residents of Zambia's cities, adequate housing remains elusive," Dr. Mwansa began. "The rapid pace of urbanization has led to the proliferation of informal settlements, characterized by inadequate housing, overcrowding, and lack of basic services."

The next slide showcased statistics highlighting the scale and severity of the housing crisis in Zambia's cities, from soaring housing prices to the prevalence of informal settlements. "The challenge of housing and slum upgrading is not just about providing shelter; it is about ensuring access to safe, affordable, and dignified housing for all residents," Dr. Mwansa continued. "It is a complex and multifaceted issue that requires coordinated action from government, private sector, and civil society."

A student raised her hand, her voice filled with concern. "How can we address the housing crisis and improve living conditions in informal settlements?"

"An excellent question," Dr. Mwansa replied, bringing up a slide illustrating strategies for housing and slum upgrading in Zambian cities. "Addressing the housing crisis requires a multi-pronged approach that combines policy interventions, community participation, and innovative financing mechanisms."

He then displayed images of housing rehabilitation projects, infrastructure upgrades, and community-led initiatives, highlighting the diverse range of interventions aimed at improving living conditions in informal settlements. "Key strategies include upgrading informal settlements through infrastructure improvements and housing rehabilitation, promoting affordable housing schemes and rental subsidies, and enhancing access to basic services such as water, sanitation, and electricity," Dr. Mwansa explained. "It also involves fostering community participation and empowerment, strengthening land tenure security, and promoting inclusive urban planning and design."

A student in the front row spoke up, her voice brimming with empathy. "How can we ensure that housing and slum upgrading initiatives are sustainable and inclusive?"

Dr. Mwansa nodded, acknowledging the importance of sustainability and inclusivity in housing interventions. "Ensuring that housing and slum upgrading initiatives are sustainable and inclusive requires a holistic and participatory approach that addresses the root causes of the housing crisis and empowers communities," he replied, transitioning to a slide showing examples of sustainable housing and slum upgrading initiatives.

"This includes integrating environmental sustainability and resilience into housing design and construction, promoting alternative building materials and green technologies, and incorporating community feedback and preferences into planning and implementation processes," Dr. Mwansa explained. "It also involves strengthening social protection mechanisms, promoting income-generating activities, and providing access to education and healthcare services."

He then displayed graphs showing the positive impact of sustainable housing and slum upgrading initiatives on various indicators, from improved living conditions to enhanced social cohesion and economic resilience. "Moreover, promoting sustainable and inclusive housing is not just about providing shelter; it is about building communities where all residents can thrive and prosper," Dr. Mwansa concluded. "By working together to address the housing crisis in Zambia's cities, we can create a future where every resident has a place to call home."

As the lecture concluded, Dr. Mwansa left the students with a final thought. "Housing is not just a basic need; it is a fundamental human right. By embracing sustainability, inclusivity, and solidarity, we can unlock the full potential of Zambia's cities and build a brighter future for all."

The students left the hall, their minds buzzing with new-found insights into the complexities of housing and slum upgrading in urban Zambia. They understood that by championing inclusive and sustainable approaches, they could contribute to building vibrant, resilient, and equitable cities across the country.

Dr. Mwansa watched them go, filled with hope for the impact they would make as future leaders and change-makers in Zambia's urban development. He knew that with their passion, determination, and commitment to social justice, they would continue to drive progress and positive change, shaping a future where every Zambian can thrive and prosper.

Urban Planning and Design in Zambia

The lecture hall transformed into a canvas of architectural blueprints and cityscapes as Dr. Mwansa delved into the intricacies of urban planning and design in Zambia. The students, captivated by the images of bustling streets and modern developments, leaned forward in anticipation, ready to explore the transformative power of thoughtful urban design.

"Good afternoon, everyone," Dr. Mwansa greeted, his voice echoing with enthusiasm and expertise. "Today, we embark on a journey through the dynamic world of urban planning and design in Zambia, and unravel the strategies for creating vibrant, livable cities."

With a click, the screen illuminated with images showcasing the evolution of urban landscapes in Zambia, from colonial-era town planning to contemporary urban developments. "Urban planning and design play a pivotal role in shaping the physical, social, and economic fabric of our cities," Dr. Mwansa began. "From the layout of streets and public spaces to the design of buildings and infrastructure, every aspect of urban design influences the quality of life and well-being of urban residents."

The next slide showcased examples of innovative urban design projects, from pedestrian-friendly streetscapes to mixed-use developments and green spaces. "Effective urban planning and design prioritize accessibility, sustainability, and inclusivity," Dr. Mwansa continued. "They create environments that are conducive to social interaction, economic activity, and environmental stewardship."

A student raised her hand, her voice filled with curiosity. "What are some of the key principles of urban planning and design that can contribute to creating more livable cities in Zambia?"

"An excellent question," Dr. Mwansa replied, bringing up a slide illustrating the principles of urban planning and design in Zambia. "Key principles include promoting compact and mixed-use development, prioritizing public transportation and non-motorized mobility, and preserving and enhancing natural and cultural heritage."

He then displayed images of walkable neighborhoods, vibrant public spaces, and sustainable infrastructure, highlighting the diverse range of approaches to urban planning and design. "Effective urban planning and design also involve promoting social inclusion and equity, fostering community participation and empowerment, and integrating climate resilience and disaster risk reduction into urban development," Dr. Mwansa explained. "It is about creating cities that are not only aesthetically pleasing but also socially inclusive, environmentally sustainable, and economically vibrant."

A student in the front row spoke up, her voice brimming with excitement. "How can we ensure that urban planning and design initiatives are responsive to the needs and aspirations of urban residents?"

Dr. Mwansa nodded, acknowledging the importance of community engagement in urban development. "Ensuring that urban planning and design initiatives are responsive and inclusive requires meaningful engagement with urban residents, stakeholders, and communities," he replied, transitioning to a slide showing examples of participatory urban planning processes.

"This includes conducting community consultations and participatory design workshops, gathering feedback and input from diverse stakeholders, and incorporating local knowledge and preferences into planning and decision-making processes," Dr. Mwansa explained. "It also involves fostering partnerships and collaboration among government agencies, private sector actors, and civil society organizations, and promoting transparency and accountability in urban governance."

He then displayed graphs showing the positive impact of participatory urban planning and design initiatives on various indicators, from social cohesion to environmental sustainability and economic prosperity. "Moreover, promoting inclusive and responsive urban planning and design is not just about creating beautiful cities; it is about building communities where all residents can thrive and prosper," Dr. Mwansa concluded. "By working together to prioritize people-centered urban development, we can create a future where every resident has the opportunity to enjoy a high quality of life and fulfill their potential."

As the lecture concluded, Dr. Mwansa left the students with a final thought. "Urban planning and design is not just a technical exercise; it is a creative and collaborative endeavor. By embracing innovation, inclusivity, and sustainability, we can unlock the full potential of Zambia's cities and build a brighter future for all."

The students left the hall, their minds buzzing with new-found insights into the transformative power of urban planning and design. They understood that by championing people-centered approaches, they could contribute to building vibrant, resilient, and equitable cities across the country.

Dr. Mwansa watched them go, filled with hope for the impact they would make as future leaders and change-makers in Zambia's urban development. He knew that with their passion, determination, and commitment to creating better cities, they would continue to drive progress and positive change, shaping a future where every Zambian can thrive and prosper.

Transportation and Mobility in Zambian Urban Areas

The lecture hall transformed into a bustling transport hub as Dr. Mwansa delved into the intricacies of transportation and mobility in Zambia's urban areas. The students, captivated by the images of busy streets and bustling terminals, leaned forward in anticipation, eager to explore the dynamics shaping movement and accessibility in the city.

"Good afternoon, everyone," Dr. Mwansa greeted, his voice resonating with authority and insight. "Today, we embark on a journey through the dynamic world of transportation and mobility in Zambia's urban areas, and unravel the strategies for enhancing connectivity and accessibility."

With a click, the screen illuminated with images showcasing the diversity of transportation modes in Zambian cities, from crowded minibuses to sleek light rail systems. "Transportation and mobility are the lifeblood of urban centers, facilitating the movement of people, goods, and services," Dr. Mwansa began. "From public transit to walking and cycling infrastructure, every aspect of transportation influences the efficiency, safety, and sustainability of urban mobility."

The next slide showcased examples of integrated transport networks, pedestrian-friendly streetscapes, and bicycle lanes, highlighting the diverse range of approaches to transportation planning and design. "Effective transportation planning and design prioritize accessibility, affordability, and sustainability," Dr. Mwansa continued. "They create environments that are conducive to active mobility, reduce congestion and pollution, and promote social inclusion and equity."

A student raised her hand, her voice tinged with curiosity. "What are some of the key challenges associated with transportation and mobility in Zambian cities?"

"An excellent question," Dr. Mwansa replied, bringing up a slide illustrating the challenges of transportation and mobility in Zambia. "Key challenges include inadequate public transportation systems, traffic congestion, road safety concerns, and lack of infrastructure for walking and cycling."

He then displayed images of congested streets, informal transport hubs, and pedestrian-unfriendly environments, highlighting the urgent need for sustainable transportation solutions. "Addressing these challenges requires a multi-pronged approach that combines infrastructure investments, policy interventions, and behavioral change," Dr. Mwansa explained. "It also involves fostering partnerships and collaboration among government agencies, private sector actors, and civil society organizations, and promoting innovation and technology in transportation planning and management."

A student in the front row spoke up, her voice filled with concern. "How can we ensure that transportation and mobility initiatives are responsive to the needs and preferences of urban residents?"

Dr. Mwansa nodded, acknowledging the importance of user-centric approaches in transportation planning. "Ensuring that transportation and mobility initiatives are responsive and inclusive requires meaningful engagement with urban residents, stakeholders, and communities," he replied, transitioning to a slide showing examples of participatory transport planning processes.

"This includes conducting surveys and focus groups to gather feedback and input from diverse user groups, analyzing travel patterns and behavior, and incorporating local knowledge and preferences into planning and decision-making processes," Dr. Mwansa explained. "It also involves promoting education and awareness campaigns on sustainable mobility options, and providing incentives for modal shift and behavior change."

He then displayed graphs showing the positive impact of participatory transport planning and design initiatives on various indicators, from reduced congestion to improved air quality and enhanced social inclusion. "Moreover, promoting sustainable and inclusive transportation and mobility is not just about improving infrastructure; it is about enhancing quality of life and well-being for all residents," Dr. Mwansa concluded. "By working together to prioritize people-centered transport solutions, we can create a future where every resident can enjoy safe, efficient, and sustainable mobility."

As the lecture concluded, Dr. Mwansa left the students with a final thought. "Transportation and mobility are not just means of getting from point A to point B; they are pathways to opportunity, connectivity, and inclusion. By embracing innovation, inclusivity, and sustainability, we can unlock the full potential of Zambia's urban areas and build a brighter future for all."

The students left the hall, their minds buzzing with newfound insights into the transformative power of transportation and mobility. They understood that by championing people-centered approaches, they could contribute to building vibrant, resilient, and equitable cities across the country.

Dr. Mwansa watched them go, filled with hope for the impact they would make as future leaders and change-makers in Zambia's urban development. He knew that with their passion, determination, and commitment to creating better cities, they would continue to drive progress and positive change, shaping a future where every Zambian can thrive and prosper.

Urban Governance in Zsmbia

The lecture hall transformed into a model city hall as Dr. Mwansa delved into the intricacies of urban governance in Zambia. The students, captivated by the images of city officials and community leaders, leaned forward in anticipation, ready to explore the mechanisms shaping decision-making and accountability in the city.

"Good afternoon, everyone," Dr. Mwansa greeted, his voice resonating with authority and insight. "Today, we delve into the dynamic world of urban governance in Zambia, and unravel the strategies for promoting transparency, participation, and effectiveness in city management."

With a click, the screen illuminated with images showcasing the diverse array of stakeholders involved in urban governance, from local authorities to community organizations. "Urban governance is the foundation of effective city management, encompassing the institutions, processes, and relationships that shape decision-making and service delivery," Dr. Mwansa began. "From city councils to neighborhood associations, every aspect of urban governance influences the quality of life and well-being of urban residents."

The next slide showcased examples of participatory budgeting, citizen engagement initiatives, and intergovernmental cooperation, highlighting the diverse range of approaches to urban governance in Zambia. "Effective urban governance prioritizes transparency, accountability, and inclusivity," Dr. Mwansa continued. "It fosters trust between government and citizens, ensures that decision-making processes are responsive to community needs, and promotes collaboration among different levels of government and stakeholders."

A student raised her hand, her voice tinged with curiosity. "What are some of the key challenges associated with urban governance in Zambia?"

"An excellent question," Dr. Mwansa replied, bringing up a slide illustrating the challenges of urban governance in Zambia. "Key challenges include limited capacity and resources at the local government level, lack of coordination among different government agencies, and weak accountability mechanisms."

He then displayed images of bureaucratic red tape, service delivery bottlenecks, and community dissatisfaction, highlighting the urgent need for improved governance structures. "Addressing these challenges requires a concerted effort to strengthen institutional capacity, enhance coordination and collaboration among government agencies, and promote transparency and accountability in decision-making processes," Dr. Mwansa explained. "It also involves empowering local authorities and communities to participate in decision-making and service delivery, and promoting innovation and technology in governance practices."

A student in the front row spoke up, her voice filled with concern. "How can we ensure that urban governance initiatives are responsive to the needs and preferences of urban residents?"

Dr. Mwansa nodded, acknowledging the importance of citizen engagement in urban governance. "Ensuring that urban governance initiatives are responsive and inclusive requires meaningful engagement with urban residents, stakeholders, and communities," he replied, transitioning to a slide showing examples of participatory governance processes.

"This includes establishing mechanisms for citizen participation and feedback, such as public forums, citizen advisory boards, and online platforms for consultation," Dr. Mwansa explained. "It also involves promoting transparency and access to information, strengthening mechanisms for public oversight and accountability, and fostering partnerships and collaboration among government agencies, civil society organizations, and the private sector."

He then displayed graphs showing the positive impact of participatory governance initiatives on various indicators, from increased citizen satisfaction to improved service delivery and social cohesion. "Moreover, promoting transparent and inclusive urban governance is not just about improving administrative efficiency; it is about building trust and social capital within communities," Dr. Mwansa concluded. "By working together to prioritize citizen participation and accountability, we can create a future where every resident has a voice in shaping their city."

As the lecture concluded, Dr. Mwansa left the students with a final thought. "Urban governance is not just about managing cities; it is about empowering communities, fostering democracy, and promoting social justice. By embracing transparency, participation, and accountability, we can unlock the full potential of Zambia's urban areas and build a brighter future for all."

The students left the hall, their minds buzzing with newfound insights into the transformative power of urban governance. They understood that by championing participatory approaches, they could contribute to building vibrant, resilient, and equitable cities across the country.

Dr. Mwansa watched them go, filled with hope for the impact they would make as future leaders and change-makers in Zambia's urban development. He knew that with their passion, determination, and commitment to creating better cities, they would continue to drive progress and positive change, shaping a future where every Zambian can thrive and prosper.

Sustainable Cities and Smart Growth in Zambia

The lecture hall morphed into a visionary cityscape as Dr. Mwansa delved into the concepts of sustainable cities and smart growth in Zambia. The students, captivated by the images of green rooftops and efficient transportation systems, leaned forward in anticipation, eager to explore the pathways to a more sustainable urban future.

"Good afternoon, everyone," Dr. Mwansa greeted, his voice filled with passion and purpose. "Today, we embark on a journey through the dynamic world of sustainable cities and smart growth in Zambia, and unravel the strategies for creating livable, resilient, and environmentally-friendly urban environments."

With a click, the screen illuminated with images showcasing the principles of sustainable urban development, from energy-efficient buildings to green spaces and eco-friendly transportation options. "Sustainable cities prioritize environmental stewardship, economic prosperity, and social equity," Dr. Mwansa began. "From green infrastructure to renewable energy systems, every aspect of urban planning and design influences the sustainability and resilience of our cities."

The next slide showcased examples of sustainable urban projects, from green buildings to urban agriculture initiatives, highlighting the diverse range of approaches to smart growth in Zambia. "Smart growth strategies promote compact, mixed-use development, efficient transportation systems, and vibrant public spaces," Dr. Mwansa continued. "They create environments that are conducive to healthy living, reduce carbon emissions, and enhance quality of life for residents."

A student raised her hand, her voice tinged with curiosity. "What are some of the key challenges associated with sustainable urban development in Zambia?"

"An excellent question," Dr. Mwansa replied, bringing up a slide illustrating the challenges of sustainable urban development in Zambia. "Key challenges include rapid urbanization, inadequate infrastructure, and limited resources for investment in sustainable technologies."

He then displayed images of urban sprawl, air pollution, and informal settlements, highlighting the urgent need for transformative action. "Addressing these challenges requires a holistic approach that integrates environmental, economic, and social considerations into urban planning and development," Dr. Mwansa explained. "It also involves fostering partnerships and collaboration among government agencies, private sector actors, and civil society organizations, and promoting innovation and technology in sustainable urban solutions."

A student in the front row spoke up, her voice filled with concern. "How can we ensure that sustainable urban development initiatives are inclusive and equitable?"

Dr. Mwansa nodded, acknowledging the importance of social equity in sustainable urban development. "Ensuring that sustainable urban development initiatives are inclusive and equitable requires meaningful engagement with diverse stakeholders, including marginalized communities and vulnerable populations," he replied, transitioning to a slide showing examples of inclusive urban planning processes.

"This includes conducting social impact assessments, addressing the needs of low-income communities, and promoting affordable housing and access to essential services," Dr. Mwansa explained. "It also involves empowering local communities to participate in decision-making and implementation processes, and ensuring that the benefits of sustainable development are shared equitably among all residents."

He then displayed graphs showing the positive impact of inclusive urban development initiatives on various indicators, from poverty reduction to social cohesion and environmental justice. "Moreover, promoting inclusive and sustainable cities is not just about improving living standards; it is about building resilient communities and fostering a sense of belonging and ownership," Dr. Mwansa concluded. "By working together to prioritize sustainability, equity, and resilience, we can create a future where every resident can thrive and prosper."

As the lecture concluded, Dr. Mwansa left the students with a final thought. "Sustainable cities are not just a vision for the future; they are a necessity for our planet and our well-being. By embracing innovation, inclusivity, and sustainability, we can unlock the full potential of Zambia's urban areas and build a brighter future for all."

The students left the hall, their minds buzzing with new-found insights into the transformative power of sustainable urban development. They understood that by championing sustainability and equity, they could contribute to building vibrant, resilient, and inclusive cities across the country.

Dr. Mwansa watched them go, filled with hope for the

impact they would make as future leaders and change-makers in Zambia's urban development. He knew that with their passion, determination, and commitment to creating better cities, they would continue to drive progress and positive change, shaping a future where every Zambian can thrive and prosper.

13

Chapter 13: Technology and Development

Role of ICT in Zambia's Development

The lecture hall hummed with anticipation as Dr. Mwansa stepped up to the podium, ready to delve into the transformative role of technology in Zambia's development. The students, eager to explore the digital frontier, leaned forward in their seats, their eyes fixed on the screen, awaiting enlightenment.

"Good afternoon, everyone," Dr. Mwansa greeted, his voice infused with enthusiasm and energy. "Today, we embark on a journey through the dynamic world of technology and development in Zambia, and unravel the ways in which information and communication technologies (ICT) are reshaping our nation's future."

With a click, the screen illuminated with images showcasing the impact of ICT on various sectors of Zambian society, from education to healthcare and beyond. "ICT has emerged as a powerful driver of socio-economic development, offering new opportunities for innovation, efficiency, and inclusion," Dr. Mwansa began. "From mobile phones to the internet, every aspect of ICT plays a crucial role in enhancing productivity, expanding access to services, and empowering individuals and communities."

The next slide showcased examples of ICT initiatives in Zambia, from e-government services to mobile banking and telemedicine, highlighting the diverse range of applications transforming lives across the country. "ICT is revolutionizing how we communicate, how we learn, and how we conduct business," Dr. Mwansa continued. "It is breaking down barriers, bridging gaps, and unlocking new pathways to progress and prosperity."

A student raised her hand, her voice tinged with curiosity. "What are some of the key challenges associated with harnessing ICT for development in Zambia?"

"An excellent question," Dr. Mwansa replied, bringing up a slide illustrating the challenges of ICT development in Zambia. "Key challenges include limited infrastructure and connectivity, high costs of access, and digital literacy gaps."

He then displayed images of rural communities without internet access, outdated technology in schools, and cyber security threats, highlighting the urgent need for concerted action. "Addressing these challenges requires a multi-faceted approach that combines infrastructure investments, policy interventions, and capacity-building initiatives," Dr. Mwansa explained. "It also involves fostering partnerships and collaboration among government, private sector, and civil society stakeholders, and promoting innovation and entrepreneurship in the ICT sector."

A student in the front row spoke up, her voice filled with concern. "How can we ensure that ICT initiatives are inclusive and accessible to all?"

Dr. Mwansa nodded, acknowledging the importance of digital inclusion in ICT development. "Ensuring that ICT initiatives are inclusive and accessible requires addressing barriers to access and participation, such as affordability, language barriers, and digital literacy," he replied, transitioning to a slide showing examples of inclusive ICT programs.

"This includes expanding broadband infrastructure to underserved areas, providing affordable devices and connectivity options, and offering digital skills training and support," Dr. Mwansa explained. "It also involves promoting content and services that are culturally relevant and locally appropriate, and ensuring that ICT policies and programs are informed by the needs and perspectives of diverse communities."

He then displayed graphs showing the positive impact of inclusive ICT initiatives on various indicators, from economic growth to social inclusion and empowerment. "Moreover, promoting inclusive and accessible ICT is not just about expanding connectivity; it is about creating opportunities for all Zambians to participate in the digital economy and society," Dr. Mwansa concluded. "By working together to prioritize digital inclusion, we can harness the full potential of ICT to drive sustainable development and build a brighter future for all."

As the lecture concluded, Dr. Mwansa left the students with a final thought. "ICT is not just a tool; it is a catalyst for change. By embracing innovation, inclusion, and collaboration, we can unlock the transformative power of technology and chart a course towards a more prosperous and equitable Zambia."

The students left the hall, their minds buzzing with new-found insights into the transformative potential of ICT. They understood that by championing digital inclusion and innovation, they could contribute to building a more connected, empowered, and prosperous Zambia for generations to come.

Dr. Mwansa watched them go, filled with hope for the impact they would make as future leaders and change-makers in Zambia's digital revolution. He knew that with their passion, determination, and commitment to harnessing technology for good, they would continue to drive progress and positive change, shaping a future where every Zambian can thrive and prosper.

Digital Divide and Inclusion in Zambia

The lecture hall pulsed with anticipation as Dr. Mwansa took center stage, ready to explore the intricacies of the digital divide and inclusion in Zambia. The students, eager to uncover the nuances of technology accessibility, leaned in closer, their eyes fixed on the screen, eager to unravel the complexities.

"Good afternoon, everyone," Dr. Mwansa greeted, his voice resonating with empathy and determination. "Today, we embark on a journey through the digital landscape of Zambia, and delve into the challenges and opportunities presented by the digital divide and the imperative of digital inclusion."

With a click, the screen illuminated with images showcasing the disparities in technology access and usage across Zambia, from urban centers to rural communities. "The digital divide refers to the gap between those who have access to information and communication technologies (ICT) and those who do not," Dr. Mwansa began. "It encompasses disparities in connectivity, affordability, digital literacy, and relevance of content and services."

The next slide displayed statistics illustrating the extent of the digital divide in Zambia, from uneven internet penetration rates to disparities in device ownership and digital skills. "The digital divide perpetuates inequalities and limits opportunities for economic and social development," Dr. Mwansa continued. "It exacerbates existing disparities in education, healthcare, and economic opportunities, and undermines efforts to build an inclusive and equitable society."

A student raised her hand, her voice tinged with concern. "What are some of the key factors contributing to the digital divide in Zambia?"

"An excellent question," Dr. Mwansa replied, bringing up a slide illustrating the drivers of the digital divide in Zambia. "Key factors include inadequate ICT infrastructure, high costs of access, limited digital literacy and skills, and lack of locally relevant content and services."

He then displayed images of remote villages without internet access, families struggling to afford smartphones, and students unable to access online learning resources, highlighting the urgent need for targeted interventions. "Addressing the digital divide requires a multi-dimensional approach that tackles barriers to access, affordability, and skills," Dr. Mwansa explained. "It also involves fostering partnerships and collaboration among government, private sector, and civil society stakeholders, and promoting innovative solutions that are tailored to the needs of underserved communities."

A student in the front row spoke up, her voice filled with determination. "How can we bridge the digital divide and ensure that all Zambians have equal opportunities to participate in the digital economy and society?"

Dr. Mwansa nodded, acknowledging the importance of collective action in bridging the digital divide. "Bridging the digital divide requires concerted efforts from all stakeholders, including government, private sector, civil society, and the international community," he replied, transitioning to a slide showing examples of digital inclusion initiatives.

"This includes investing in ICT infrastructure and expanding broadband connectivity to underserved areas, subsidizing access to devices and connectivity for low-income households, and providing digital skills training and support," Dr. Mwansa explained. "It also involves promoting locally relevant content and services, fostering digital entrepreneurship, and creating an enabling policy and regulatory environment."

He then displayed graphs showing the positive impact of digital inclusion initiatives on various indicators, from economic growth to social inclusion and empowerment. "Moreover, bridging the digital divide is not just about expanding access to technology; it is about creating opportunities for all Zambians to participate in the digital economy and society," Dr. Mwansa concluded. "By working together to prioritize digital inclusion, we can ensure that no one is left behind in the digital age."

As the lecture concluded, Dr. Mwansa left the students with a final thought. "The digital divide may be daunting, but it is not insurmountable. By embracing innovation, collaboration, and inclusion, we can bridge the gap and unlock the full potential of technology to drive progress and prosperity for all Zambians."

The students left the hall, their minds buzzing with new-found insights into the complexities of the digital divide and the imperative of digital inclusion. They understood that by championing digital equity and empowerment, they could contribute to building a more connected, inclusive, and prosperous Zambia for generations to come.

Dr. Mwansa watched them go, filled with hope for the impact they would make as future leaders and change-makers in Zambia's digital transformation. He knew that with their passion, determination, and commitment to bridging the digital divide, they would continue to drive progress and positive change, shaping a future where every Zambian can thrive and prosper.

Innovation and Entrepreneurship in Zambia

The lecture hall buzzed with excitement as Dr. Mwansa stepped onto the stage, ready to explore the dynamic world of innovation and entrepreneurship in Zambia. The students, eager to dive into the realm of creativity and enterprise, leaned forward in anticipation, their eyes gleaming with curiosity.

"Good afternoon, everyone," Dr. Mwansa greeted, his voice filled with enthusiasm and energy. "Today, we embark on a journey through the landscape of innovation and entrepreneurship in Zambia, and uncover the transformative power of creativity, ingenuity, and enterprise."

With a click, the screen illuminated with images showcasing the vibrancy of Zambia's entrepreneurial ecosystem, from bustling marketplaces to cutting-edge startups and innovative social enterprises. "Innovation and entrepreneurship are driving forces of economic growth, job creation, and social change," Dr. Mwansa began. "They empower individuals to turn ideas into reality, create value, and make a positive impact on their communities and the world."

The next slide showcased examples of innovative startups and entrepreneurs in Zambia, from tech pioneers to social innovators, highlighting the diverse range of ventures fueling the country's progress. "Innovation knows no bounds," Dr. Mwansa continued. "From technology to agriculture, healthcare to renewable energy, entrepreneurs are pioneering new solutions to old challenges and transforming industries in the process."

A student raised her hand, her voice tinged with curiosity. "What are some of the key factors driving innovation and entrepreneurship in Zambia?"

"An excellent question," Dr. Mwansa replied, bringing up a slide illustrating the drivers of innovation and entrepreneurship in Zambia. "Key factors include access to education and skills development, supportive policy and regulatory frameworks, access to finance and market opportunities, and a culture of creativity and risk-taking."

He then displayed images of innovation hubs, incubators, and accelerators, highlighting the ecosystem of support available to aspiring entrepreneurs across the country. "Zambia is home to a vibrant community of innovators and entrepreneurs who are harnessing the power of technology, creativity, and collaboration to tackle some of our most pressing challenges," Dr. Mwansa explained. "From fintech startups to agri-tech ventures, they are driving innovation-led growth and creating opportunities for all Zambians to prosper."

A student in the front row spoke up, her voice filled with determination. "How can we foster a culture of innovation and entrepreneurship in Zambia and support aspiring entrepreneurs?"

Dr. Mwansa nodded, acknowledging the importance of nurturing a conducive environment for innovation and entrepreneurship. "Fostering a culture of innovation and entrepreneurship requires a multi-faceted approach that combines education, mentorship, access to finance, and supportive policy frameworks," he replied, transitioning to a slide showing examples of initiatives supporting entrepreneurship.

"This includes promoting STEM education and skills development, providing mentorship and training for aspiring entrepreneurs, facilitating access to finance and market opportunities, and creating an enabling policy environment that incentivizes innovation and entrepreneurship," Dr. Mwansa explained. "It also involves building networks and partnerships that connect entrepreneurs with resources, expertise, and market opportunities."

He then displayed graphs showing the positive impact of entrepreneurship on various indicators, from job creation to economic growth and social inclusion. "Moreover, entrepreneurship is not just about starting businesses; it is about solving problems, creating value, and making a difference in the world," Dr. Mwansa concluded. "By supporting and celebrating our innovators and entrepreneurs, we can unlock the full potential of Zambia's creative and entrepreneurial spirit and build a brighter future for all."

As the lecture concluded, Dr. Mwansa left the students with a final thought. "Innovation and entrepreneurship are not just buzzwords; they are pathways to progress and prosperity. By embracing creativity, collaboration, and resilience, we can unleash the power of entrepreneurship to drive positive change and build a better Zambia for generations to come."

The students left the hall, their minds buzzing with new-found inspiration and determination. They understood that by championing innovation and entrepreneurship, they could contribute to building a more dynamic, inclusive, and prosperous Zambia for all its people.

Dr. Mwansa watched them go, filled with hope for the impact they would make as future innovators, entrepreneurs, and change-makers in Zambia's journey towards a brighter future. He knew that with their passion, determination, and commitment to turning ideas into action, they would continue to drive progress and positive change, shaping a future where every Zambian can thrive and prosper.

E-Governance and Digital Services in Zambia

The lecture hall crackled with anticipation as Dr. Mwansa stepped onto the stage, ready to delve into the realm of e-governance and digital services in Zambia. The students, eager to explore the intersection of technology and governance, leaned forward in their seats, their eyes shining with curiosity and excitement.

"Good afternoon, everyone," Dr. Mwansa greeted, his voice infused with enthusiasm and purpose. "Today, we embark on a journey through the landscape of e-governance and digital services in Zambia, and unravel the transformative potential of technology in shaping the future of governance and public service delivery."

With a click, the screen illuminated with images showcasing the digital transformation taking place across Zambia, from online government portals to mobile-based service delivery platforms. "E-governance encompasses the use of information and communication technologies to enhance the efficiency, transparency, and accountability of government processes and services," Dr. Mwansa began. "It empowers citizens to access government information and services anytime, anywhere, and fosters greater citizen engagement and participation in the governance process."

The next slide showcased examples of e-governance initiatives in Zambia, from online tax filing systems to digital citizen ID cards, highlighting the diverse range of services available to citizens at their fingertips. "Digital services have the power to streamline bureaucratic processes, reduce corruption, and improve the overall quality and accessibility of public services," Dr. Mwansa continued. "They enable governments to deliver services more efficiently, respond to citizen needs more effectively, and foster greater trust and confidence in public institutions."

A student raised her hand, her voice tinged with curiosity. "What are some of the key benefits and challenges of implementing e-governance initiatives in Zambia?"

"An excellent question," Dr. Mwansa replied, bringing up a slide illustrating the benefits and challenges of e-governance in Zambia. "Key benefits include improved service delivery, enhanced transparency and accountability, increased citizen engagement and participation, and greater cost savings and efficiency gains."

He then displayed images of citizens accessing government services online, submitting feedback through digital platforms, and participating in virtual town hall meetings, highlighting the transformative impact of e-governance on governance processes and citizen-state relations. "However, implementing e-governance initiatives also presents challenges, such as digital literacy gaps, infrastructure limitations, data privacy and security concerns, and institutional resistance to change," Dr. Mwansa explained. "Addressing these challenges requires a concerted effort from government, civil society, and the private sector to build the necessary capacity, infrastructure, and regulatory frameworks to support e-governance initiatives."

A student in the front row spoke up, her voice filled with determination. "How can we ensure that e-governance initiatives are inclusive and accessible to all Zambians, including those in rural and marginalized communities?"

Dr. Mwansa nodded, acknowledging the importance of digital inclusion in e-governance initiatives. "Ensuring that e-governance initiatives are inclusive and accessible to all Zambians requires addressing barriers to access, affordability, and digital literacy," he replied, transitioning to a slide showing examples of initiatives promoting digital inclusion.

"This includes investing in digital infrastructure and connectivity in underserved areas, providing training and support for digital skills development, and designing user-friendly digital platforms that are accessible to people with diverse needs and abilities," Dr. Mwansa explained. "It also involves engaging with communities to understand their specific needs and preferences, and co-creating solutions that meet those needs."

He then displayed graphs showing the positive impact of e-governance initiatives on various indicators, from citizen satisfaction to government efficiency and transparency. "Moreover, e-governance is not just about digitizing existing processes; it is about reimagining governance for the digital age," Dr. Mwansa concluded. "By harnessing the power of technology to empower citizens, strengthen institutions, and promote good governance, we can build a more inclusive, responsive, and accountable government that works for all Zambians."

As the lecture concluded, Dr. Mwansa left the students with a final thought. "E-governance holds the promise of a more transparent, efficient, and accountable government that serves the needs of all citizens. By embracing innovation, collaboration, and inclusion, we can unlock the full potential of technology to transform governance and build a better Zambia for generations to come."

The students left the hall, their minds buzzing with new-found insights into the potential of e-governance to drive positive change and innovation in Zambia. They understood that by championing digital transformation and citizen engagement, they could contribute to building a more responsive, inclusive, and accountable government for all Zambians.

Dr. Mwansa watched them go, filled with hope for the impact they would make as future leaders and change-makers in Zambia's journey towards digital governance. He knew that with their passion, determination, and commitment to harnessing technology for good, they would continue to drive progress and positive change, shaping a future where every Zambian can participate fully in the governance process and thrive.

Technology in Education and Health in Zambia

The lecture hall hummed with anticipation as Dr. Mwansa took center stage, ready to explore the transformative role of technology in education and healthcare in Zambia. The students, eager to uncover the potential of innovation in these critical sectors, leaned forward in their seats, their eyes bright with curiosity and excitement.

"Good afternoon, everyone," Dr. Mwansa greeted, his voice resonating with enthusiasm and purpose. "Today, we embark on a journey through the intersection of technology, education, and healthcare in Zambia, and delve into the profound impact of innovation on learning and well-being."

With a click, the screen illuminated with images showcasing the innovative use of technology in classrooms and clinics across Zambia, from interactive learning platforms to telemedicine services. "Technology has the power to revolutionize education and healthcare, making them more accessible, equitable, and effective," Dr. Mwansa began. "It enables learners to access quality education regardless of their location, and patients to receive timely healthcare services, even in remote areas."

The next slide showcased examples of technology-driven initiatives in education and healthcare in Zambia, from e-learning platforms to mobile health apps, highlighting the diverse range of solutions available to improve access and outcomes. "In education, technology enhances learning experiences, promotes digital literacy, and expands access to educational resources and opportunities," Dr. Mwansa continued. "In healthcare, it facilitates remote consultations, health monitoring, and disease management, improving access to quality care and empowering individuals to take charge of their health."

A student raised her hand, her voice tinged with curiosity. "What are some of the key benefits and challenges of integrating technology into education and healthcare in Zambia?"

"An excellent question," Dr. Mwansa replied, bringing up a slide illustrating the benefits and challenges of technology integration. "Key benefits include increased access to educational and healthcare resources, improved learning and health outcomes, enhanced efficiency and cost-effectiveness, and greater patient engagement and empowerment."

He then displayed images of students participating in virtual classrooms, and patients accessing telemedicine services on their smartphones, illustrating the transformative impact of technology on education and healthcare delivery. "However, integrating technology into education and healthcare also presents challenges, such as infrastructure limitations, digital literacy gaps, data privacy and security concerns, and resistance to change," Dr. Mwansa explained. "Addressing these challenges requires a holistic approach that addresses technical, socio-economic, and cultural factors, and involves collaboration among government, private sector, and civil society stakeholders."

A student in the front row spoke up, her voice filled with determination. "How can we ensure that technology-driven initiatives in education and healthcare are inclusive and accessible to all Zambians, especially those in rural and marginalized communities?"

Dr. Mwansa nodded, acknowledging the importance of digital inclusion in technology-driven initiatives. "Ensuring that technology-driven initiatives in education and healthcare are inclusive and accessible to all Zambians requires addressing barriers to access, affordability, and digital literacy," he replied, transitioning to a slide showing examples of initiatives promoting digital inclusion.

"This includes investing in digital infrastructure and connectivity in underserved areas, providing training and support for digital skills development, and designing user-friendly digital platforms that are accessible to people with diverse needs and abilities," Dr. Mwansa explained. "It also involves engaging with communities to understand their specific needs and preferences, and co-creating solutions that meet those needs."

He then displayed graphs showing the positive impact of technology-driven initiatives on various indicators, from academic performance to healthcare outcomes and patient satisfaction. "Moreover, technology is not a panacea; it is a tool that complements and enhances human efforts in education and healthcare," Dr. Mwansa concluded. "By harnessing the power of technology to empower learners and patients, we can build a more inclusive, resilient, and healthy society that benefits all Zambians."

As the lecture concluded, Dr. Mwansa left the students with a final thought. "Technology has the power to transform education and healthcare, making them more accessible, equitable, and effective. By embracing innovation, collaboration, and inclusion, we can unlock the full potential of technology to build a brighter future for all Zambians."

The students left the hall, their minds buzzing with newfound insights into the transformative potential of technology in education and healthcare. They understood that by championing innovation and digital inclusion, they could contribute to building a more equitable, resilient, and healthy Zambia for generations to come.

Dr. Mwansa watched them go, filled with hope for the impact they would make as future leaders and change-makers in Zambia's journey towards a digital future. He knew that with their passion, determination, and commitment to harnessing technology for good, they would continue to drive progress and positive change, shaping a future where every Zambian can access quality education and healthcare, regardless of their circumstances.

Future Trends and Prospects for Zambia

The anticipation in the lecture hall was palpable as Dr. Mwansa stepped onto the stage, ready to explore the future trends and prospects for technology in Zambia. The students, eager to peer into the crystal ball of innovation, leaned forward in their seats, their eyes alight with curiosity and anticipation.

"Good afternoon, everyone," Dr. Mwansa greeted, his voice brimming with excitement and optimism. "Today, we embark on a journey into the future of technology in Zambia, and explore the trends and opportunities that lie ahead."

With a click, the screen illuminated with images depicting futuristic technologies and digital advancements, from artificial intelligence to blockchain, from virtual reality to the Internet of Things. "The future of technology in Zambia is filled with boundless possibilities," Dr. Mwansa began. "As we stand on the cusp of a new era of innovation, it is essential to envision the trends and opportunities that will shape our digital landscape in the years to come."

The next slide showcased examples of emerging technologies and their potential applications in Zambia, from precision agriculture to telemedicine, from smart cities to digital finance, highlighting the transformative impact they could have on various sectors of the economy. "Emerging technologies have the power to revolutionize how we live, work, and interact with the world around us," Dr. Mwansa continued. "They offer new opportunities for economic growth, social development, and environmental sustainability, and have the potential to address some of our most pressing challenges."

A student raised her hand, her voice tinged with curiosity. "What are some of the key trends shaping the future of technology in Zambia?"

"An excellent question," Dr. Mwansa replied, bringing up a slide illustrating the key trends shaping the future of technology. "Key trends include the proliferation of mobile and internet connectivity, the rise of digital platforms and ecosystems, the increasing adoption of cloud computing and big data analytics, and the growing importance of cybersecurity and data privacy."

He then displayed images of interconnected devices and smart cities, illustrating the transformative potential of these trends on Zambia's digital landscape. "Moreover, the future of technology in Zambia is also shaped by broader global trends, such as the Fourth Industrial Revolution, the shift towards a digital economy, and the growing focus on sustainable development and social inclusion," Dr. Mwansa explained. "By aligning our strategies and investments with these trends, we can harness the full potential of technology to drive inclusive growth, promote social development, and build a more resilient and sustainable future for all Zambians."

A student in the front row spoke up, her voice filled with determination. "How can we ensure that Zambia remains at the forefront of technological innovation and harnesses the full potential of emerging technologies for the benefit of all its citizens?"

Dr. Mwansa nodded, acknowledging the importance of proactive leadership and collaboration in driving technological innovation. "Ensuring that Zambia remains at the forefront of technological innovation requires a concerted effort from government, private sector, academia, and civil society," he replied, transitioning to a slide showing examples of initiatives promoting innovation and collaboration.

"This includes investing in research and development, fostering a culture of innovation and entrepreneurship, promoting digital literacy and skills development, and creating an enabling policy and regulatory environment that supports innovation and investment," Dr. Mwansa explained. "It also involves building partnerships and collaborations that leverage the strengths and resources of all stakeholders to address common challenges and seize shared opportunities."

He then displayed graphs showing the potential impact of technological innovation on various sectors of the economy, from agriculture to healthcare, from education to energy. "Moreover, the future of technology in Zambia is not predetermined; it is shaped by the choices and actions we take today," Dr. Mwansa concluded. "By embracing innovation, collaboration, and inclusion, we can unlock the full potential of technology to build a brighter future for all Zambians."

As the lecture concluded, Dr. Mwansa left the students with a final thought. "The future of technology in Zambia is filled with promise and potential. By embracing emerging technologies and harnessing their transformative power, we can create new opportunities, address persistent challenges, and build a more prosperous, inclusive, and sustainable Zambia for generations to come."

The students left the hall, their minds buzzing with excitement and inspiration for the possibilities that lie ahead. They understood that by embracing innovation and collaboration, they could contribute to shaping a future where technology serves as a powerful force for positive change and progress in Zambia.

Dr. Mwansa watched them go, filled with hope for the impact they would make as future innovators, entrepreneurs, and leaders in Zambia's journey towards a digital future. He knew that with their passion, determination, and commitment to harnessing technology for good, they would continue to drive progress and shape a future where every Zambian can thrive and prosper in the digital age.

14

Chapter 14: Development Policy and Planning

Policy Formulation and Analysis in Zambia

In a room bathed in soft light, Dr. Mwansa stood at the front, ready to unravel the intricate dance of policy formulation and analysis in Zambia. The students, perched on the edge of their seats, their minds poised to absorb knowledge, awaited eagerly for the discourse to unfold.

"Good afternoon, everyone," Dr. Mwansa greeted, his voice carrying a tone of scholarly authority. "Today, we embark on a journey through the labyrinth of policy formulation and analysis in Zambia, where the decisions of today shape the trajectory of our nation's tomorrow."

With a click, the projector illuminated the screen with a montage of charts and graphs, showcasing the complexities of policy formulation and analysis. "Policy formulation is the process by which governments identify problems, develop solutions, and implement courses of action to address societal challenges," Dr. Mwansa elucidated. "It requires a deep understanding of the socio-economic context, stakeholder engagement, evidence-based research, and strategic foresight."

The next slide depicted the myriad factors that influence policy formulation in Zambia, from political dynamics to economic trends, from social issues to environmental concerns. "Policy analysis, on the other hand, involves evaluating the effectiveness, efficiency, and equity of policies," Dr. Mwansa continued. "It requires rigorous research, data analysis, stakeholder consultation, and critical thinking to assess the impacts and outcomes of policies on different segments of society."

A student raised her hand, her voice tinged with curiosity. "What are some of the key challenges and opportunities in policy formulation and analysis in Zambia?"

"An excellent question," Dr. Mwansa replied, bringing up a slide illustrating the challenges and opportunities. "Key challenges include limited capacity and resources, political interference, bureaucratic inertia, data gaps, and stakeholder conflicts."

He then displayed images of policymakers grappling with complex issues, stakeholders engaged in heated debates, and researchers poring over mountains of data, highlighting the formidable obstacles that must be overcome in the policy process. "However, amidst these challenges lie opportunities for innovation, collaboration, and positive change," Dr. Mwansa explained. "By leveraging technology, fostering partnerships, promoting evidence-based decision-making, and enhancing transparency and accountability, we can strengthen the policy process and improve the quality of governance in Zambia."

A student in the front row spoke up, her voice filled with

determination. "How can we ensure that policy formulation and analysis in Zambia are inclusive and responsive to the needs of all citizens?"

Dr. Mwansa nodded, acknowledging the importance of inclusive policymaking in addressing the diverse needs and priorities of Zambia's population. "Ensuring that policy formulation and analysis are inclusive and responsive requires engaging with a wide range of stakeholders, including civil society organizations, private sector actors, academia, and marginalized communities," he replied, transitioning to a slide showing examples of inclusive policymaking initiatives.

"This includes conducting robust consultations, incorporating diverse perspectives and voices, and prioritizing the needs of vulnerable and marginalized groups," Dr. Mwansa explained. "It also involves promoting transparency and accountability in the policy process, ensuring that decisions are based on evidence and guided by principles of equity and social justice."

He then displayed graphs showing the potential impact of inclusive policymaking on various indicators, from poverty reduction to social cohesion, from economic growth to environmental sustainability. "Moreover, inclusive policymaking is not just a moral imperative; it is also essential for achieving sustainable development and building a more resilient and prosperous Zambia for all," Dr. Mwansa concluded. "By embracing diversity, promoting dialogue, and fostering collaboration, we can unlock the full potential of policymaking to drive positive change and improve the lives of all Zambians."

As the lecture concluded, Dr. Mwansa left the students with a final thought. "Policy formulation and analysis are at the heart of governance, shaping the policies and decisions that affect every aspect of our lives. By embracing innovation, collaboration, and inclusion, we can strengthen the policy process and build a more prosperous, equitable, and sustainable Zambia for generations to come."

The students left the room, their minds buzzing with newfound insights into the intricacies of policymaking in Zambia. They understood that by championing evidence-based decision-making and inclusive governance, they could contribute to shaping policies that address the needs and aspirations of all Zambians.

Dr. Mwansa watched them go, filled with hope for the impact they would make as future policymakers, analysts, and leaders in Zambia's journey towards a brighter future. He knew that with their passion, determination, and commitment to good governance, they would continue to drive progress and shape policies that improve the lives of all Zambians, today and tomorrow.

Development Planning Models for Zambia

In the hushed ambiance of the lecture hall, Dr. Mwansa assumed the podium, ready to navigate the intricate landscape of development planning models for Zambia. Eager minds, poised for enlightenment, awaited the unveiling of Zambia's strategic roadmap.

"Good afternoon, everyone," Dr. Mwansa greeted, his voice resonating with authority and clarity. "Today, we embark on a journey through the realm of development planning models in Zambia, where aspirations are transformed into actionable strategies for progress and prosperity."

With a click, the screen illuminated with a montage of charts and diagrams, illustrating the diverse array of development planning models utilized in Zambia. "Development planning is the process by which governments set goals, identify priorities, and allocate resources to achieve sustainable development," Dr. Mwansa elucidated. "It requires foresight, collaboration, and adaptability to navigate the complexities of socio-economic dynamics and global trends."

The next slide showcased the various development planning models employed in Zambia, from long-term national development plans to sectoral strategies and regional development frameworks. "Each model offers a unique approach to addressing Zambia's development challenges and opportunities," Dr. Mwansa continued. "From top-down approaches that prioritize centralized decision-making to bottom-up approaches that empower local communities, the choice of planning model depends on a range of factors, including political context, institutional capacity, and stakeholder preferences."

A student raised her hand, her voice tinged with curiosity. "What are some of the key considerations in selecting and implementing development planning models in Zambia?"

"An excellent question," Dr. Mwansa replied, bringing up a slide illustrating the key considerations. "Key considerations include alignment with national development priorities, stakeholder participation and ownership, integration of cross-cutting issues such as gender and environmental sustainability, and flexibility to adapt to changing circumstances."

He then displayed images of policymakers deliberating over development plans, stakeholders engaging in consultations, and communities participating in decision-making processes, highlighting the collaborative and dynamic nature of development planning in Zambia. "Moreover, successful development planning requires effective coordination, monitoring, and evaluation to ensure that goals are achieved, resources are utilized efficiently, and impacts are maximized," Dr. Mwansa explained. "It also involves fostering partnerships and collaborations among government, private sector, civil society, and development partners to mobilize resources, share expertise, and leverage synergies."

A student in the front row spoke up, her voice filled with determination. "How can we ensure that development planning in Zambia is responsive to the needs and aspirations of all citizens?"

Dr. Mwansa nodded, acknowledging the importance of inclusive and participatory development planning in fostering ownership and sustainability. "Ensuring that development planning is responsive to the needs and aspirations of all citizens requires engaging with a wide range of stakeholders, including marginalized communities, youth, women, and persons with disabilities," he replied, transitioning to a slide showing examples of inclusive development planning processes.

"This includes conducting consultations, surveys, and focus group discussions to gather inputs and feedback, as well as incorporating mechanisms for citizen engagement and feedback throughout the planning cycle," Dr. Mwansa explained. "It also involves promoting transparency, accountability, and accessibility in the planning process, ensuring that information is readily available and understandable to all stakeholders."

He then displayed graphs showing the potential impact of inclusive development planning on various indicators, from poverty reduction to social cohesion, from economic growth to environmental sustainability. "Moreover, inclusive development planning is not just a moral imperative; it is also essential for achieving sustainable development and building a more resilient and prosperous Zambia for all," Dr. Mwansa concluded. "By embracing diversity, promoting dialogue, and fostering collaboration, we can unlock the full potential of development planning to drive positive change and improve the lives of all Zambians."

As the lecture concluded, Dr. Mwansa left the students with a final thought. "Development planning is the compass that guides our journey towards a brighter future. By embracing innovation, collaboration, and inclusion, we can chart a course that leads to prosperity, equity, and sustainability for all Zambians."

The students left the room, their minds buzzing with new-found insights into the intricacies of development planning in Zambia. They understood that by championing inclusive and participatory approaches, they could contribute to shaping a future where development planning is a catalyst for positive change and progress in Zambia.

Dr. Mwansa watched them go, filled with hope for the impact they would make as future planners, policymakers, and leaders in Zambia's journey towards a brighter tomorrow. He knew that with their passion, determination, and commitment to inclusive development, they would continue to drive progress and shape policies that improve the lives of all Zambians, today and in the years to come.

Monitoring and Evaluation in Zambian Development

In the serene atmosphere of the lecture hall, Dr. Mwansa took center stage, poised to delve into the critical realm of monitoring and evaluation in Zambian development. An air of anticipation enveloped the room as eager minds awaited the unveiling of Zambia's evaluative landscape.

"Good afternoon, everyone," Dr. Mwansa greeted, his voice resonating with authority and gravitas. "Today, we embark on a journey through the realm of monitoring and evaluation in Zambian development, where progress is measured, lessons are learned, and strategies are refined."

With a click, the screen illuminated with a montage of graphs and charts, showcasing the diverse array of monitoring and evaluation mechanisms employed in Zambia. "Monitoring and evaluation are essential components of the development process, providing insights into the effectiveness, efficiency, and impact of policies, programs, and projects," Dr. Mwansa elucidated. "They enable policymakers, practitioners, and stakeholders to assess progress, identify challenges, and make informed decisions to improve development outcomes."

The next slide showcased the various monitoring and evaluation tools and methodologies utilized in Zambia, from performance indicators and baseline surveys to impact assessments and outcome evaluations. "Each tool offers a unique perspective on the development process, providing valuable information for decision-making and accountability," Dr. Mwansa continued. "From quantitative data that measure outputs and outcomes to qualitative insights that capture the voices and experiences of beneficiaries, monitoring and evaluation help to paint a comprehensive picture of Zambia's development landscape."

A student raised her hand, her voice tinged with curiosity. "What are some of the key challenges and opportunities in monitoring and evaluation in Zambia?"

"An excellent question," Dr. Mwansa replied, bringing up a slide illustrating the key challenges and opportunities. "Key challenges include limited capacity and resources, data gaps and quality issues, coordination and collaboration among stakeholders, and ensuring that findings are used to inform decision-making."

He then displayed images of evaluators grappling with complex datasets, policymakers reviewing evaluation reports, and communities participating in feedback mechanisms, highlighting the formidable obstacles that must be overcome in the monitoring and evaluation process. "However, amidst these challenges lie opportunities for innovation, learning, and improvement," Dr. Mwansa explained. "By investing in capacity building, strengthening data systems, promoting transparency and accountability, and fostering a culture of learning and adaptation, we can enhance the effectiveness and impact of monitoring and evaluation in Zambia."

A student in the front row spoke up, her voice filled with determination. "How can we ensure that monitoring and evaluation in Zambia are responsive to the needs and aspirations of all citizens?"

Dr. Mwansa nodded, acknowledging the importance of participatory and inclusive monitoring and evaluation in promoting ownership and accountability. "Ensuring that monitoring and evaluation are responsive to the needs and aspirations of all citizens requires engaging with a wide range of stakeholders, including communities, civil society organizations, and marginalized groups," he replied, transitioning to a slide showing examples of participatory monitoring and evaluation approaches.

"This includes involving stakeholders in the design, implementation, and interpretation of evaluations, as well as providing opportunities for feedback and dialogue throughout the process," Dr. Mwansa explained. "It also involves promoting transparency, accessibility, and cultural sensitivity in monitoring and evaluation activities, ensuring that findings are communicated in a clear, timely, and understandable manner to all stakeholders."

He then displayed graphs showing the potential impact of participatory monitoring and evaluation on various indicators, from program effectiveness to social inclusion, from accountability to empowerment. "Moreover, participatory monitoring and evaluation is not just a technical exercise; it is also a means of promoting democratic governance, social justice, and human rights," Dr. Mwansa concluded. "By embracing diversity, promoting dialogue, and fostering collaboration, we can unlock the full potential of monitoring and evaluation to drive positive change and improve the lives of all Zambians."

As the lecture concluded, Dr. Mwansa left the students with a final thought. "Monitoring and evaluation are the compass and map that guide our journey towards a brighter future. By embracing innovation, collaboration, and inclusion, we can navigate the challenges and opportunities of development and build a more resilient, prosperous, and equitable Zambia for all."

The students left the room, their minds buzzing with newfound insights into the intricacies of monitoring and evaluation in Zambia. They understood that by championing participatory and inclusive approaches, they could contribute to shaping a future where monitoring and evaluation serve as powerful tools for positive change and progress in Zambia.

Dr. Mwansa watched them go, filled with hope for the impact they would make as future evaluators, policymakers, and leaders in Zambia's journey towards a brighter tomorrow. He knew that with their passion, determination, and commitment to inclusive development, they would continue to drive progress and shape policies that improve the lives of all Zambians, today and in the years to come.

International Development Agencies and Zambia

In the quiet ambiance of the lecture hall, Dr. Mwansa took his place at the lectern, poised to explore the intricate relationship between international development agencies and Zambia. The anticipation in the room was palpable as eager minds awaited the unveiling of Zambia's engagement with the global development community.

"Good afternoon, everyone," Dr. Mwansa greeted, his voice projecting confidence and authority. "Today, we embark on a journey through the complex terrain of Zambia's interactions with international development agencies, where partnerships are forged, resources mobilized, and expertise shared."

With a click, the screen came to life, displaying a montage of logos representing various international development agencies. "International development agencies play a crucial role in supporting Zambia's development goals, providing financial assistance, technical expertise, and policy advice," Dr. Mwansa elucidated. "From multilateral institutions like the World

Bank and the United Nations to bilateral donors such as the United States Agency for International Development (USAID) and the United Kingdom's Department for International Development (DFID), these agencies contribute to Zambia's efforts to address key development challenges and achieve sustainable development."

The next slide showcased the diverse array of initiatives and programs supported by international development agencies in Zambia, from infrastructure projects and social welfare programs to capacity-building initiatives and policy reforms. "Each agency brings its own priorities, expertise, and resources to the table, creating opportunities for collaboration and innovation," Dr. Mwansa continued. "Through strategic partnerships and mutual cooperation, Zambia can leverage the strengths of international development agencies to maximize the impact of development interventions and achieve sustainable outcomes."

A student raised her hand, her voice tinged with curiosity. "What are some of the key benefits and challenges of partnering with international development agencies?"

"An excellent question," Dr. Mwansa replied, bringing up a slide illustrating the key benefits and challenges. "Key benefits include access to financial resources, technical expertise, and global best practices, as well as opportunities for networking, learning, and capacity building."

He then displayed images of Zambian officials engaging with representatives of international development agencies, stakeholders collaborating on joint initiatives, and communities benefiting from development projects, highlighting the positive impacts of partnership and cooperation. "However, partnering with international development agencies also presents challenges, including coordination and alignment with national priorities, ownership and sustainability of initiatives, and potential risks of dependency and aid conditionality," Dr. Mwansa explained. "It is essential for Zambia to navigate these challenges effectively, ensuring that partnerships are strategic, transparent, and accountable, and that they contribute to the long-term development objectives of the country."

A student in the front row spoke up, her voice filled with determination. "How can Zambia maximize the benefits of partnering with international development agencies while mitigating the risks?"

Dr. Mwansa nodded, acknowledging the importance of strategic and principled engagement with international development agencies in achieving sustainable development outcomes. "Maximizing the benefits of partnering with international development agencies requires Zambia to adopt a strategic and coordinated approach," he replied, transitioning to a slide showing examples of best practices in partnership management.

"This includes aligning development priorities with international agendas, promoting ownership and leadership at the national level, and ensuring that partnerships are based on principles of mutual respect, equity, and accountability," Dr. Mwansa explained. "It also involves fostering dialogue, transparency, and inclusivity in decision-making processes, as well as building the capacity of local institutions and stakeholders to effectively engage with international partners."

He then displayed graphs showing the potential impact of strategic partnership management on various indicators, from program effectiveness to institutional capacity building, from stakeholder satisfaction to sustainable development outcomes. "Moreover, strategic partnership management is not just about achieving short-term objectives; it is also about building lasting relationships and fostering a culture of collaboration and trust," Dr. Mwansa concluded. "By embracing diversity, promoting dialogue, and fostering collaboration, Zambia can unlock the full potential of partnerships with international development agencies to drive positive change and improve the lives of all Zambians."

As the lecture concluded, Dr. Mwansa left the students with a final thought. "Partnerships with international development agencies are a cornerstone of Zambia's development efforts. By embracing innovation, collaboration, and inclusion, we can harness the collective power of the global community to build a more resilient, prosperous, and sustainable Zambia for all."

The students left the room, their minds buzzing with new-found insights into the complexities of Zambia's engagement with international development agencies. They understood that by championing strategic and principled partnerships, they could contribute to shaping a future where Zambia's development aspirations are realized through collaboration and cooperation with the global community.

Dr. Mwansa watched them go, filled with hope for the impact they would make as future leaders, policymakers, and changemakers in Zambia's journey towards a brighter tomorrow. He knew that with their passion, determination, and commitment to inclusive development, they would continue to drive progress and shape policies that improve the lives of all Zambians, today and in the years to come.

National Development Plans of Zambia

In the serene setting of the lecture hall, Dr. Mwansa assumed the lectern, ready to delve into the intricate landscape of Zambia's national development plans. Eager minds, poised for enlightenment, awaited the unveiling of Zambia's strategic roadmap for progress and prosperity.

"Good afternoon, everyone," Dr. Mwansa greeted, his voice commanding attention and respect. "Today, we embark on a journey through the realm of Zambia's national development plans, where aspirations are translated into action, and dreams into reality."

With a click, the screen illuminated with a montage of images showcasing Zambia's diverse landscapes, vibrant communities, and dynamic economy. "National development plans serve as blueprints for Zambia's development journey, providing a comprehensive framework for setting goals, identifying priorities, and mobilizing resources," Dr. Mwansa elucidated. "They guide the allocation of financial resources, the formulation of policies, and the implementation of programs aimed at achieving sustainable development and improving the well-being of all Zambians."

The next slide showcased Zambia's history of national development planning, from its early post-independence plans to its current long-term vision for the future. "Since gaining independence in 1964, Zambia has embarked on a series of national development plans, each reflecting the country's evolving socio-economic context, political priorities, and development aspirations," Dr. Mwansa continued. "These plans have laid the foundation for progress in key areas such as infrastructure development, social welfare, and economic diversification, while also addressing emerging challenges and opportunities."

A student raised her hand, her voice tinged with curiosity. "What are some of the key features and objectives of Zambia's national development plans?"

"An excellent question," Dr. Mwansa replied, bringing up a slide illustrating the key features and objectives. "Zambia's national development plans typically include a vision statement that articulates the country's long-term development goals, as well as a set of strategic objectives and priority areas for action."

He then displayed images of policymakers deliberating over development plans, stakeholders collaborating on implementation strategies, and communities benefiting from development projects, highlighting the inclusive and participatory nature of Zambia's planning process. "Moreover, Zambia's national development plans emphasize the principles of inclusivity, sustainability, and resilience, recognizing the importance of engaging with a wide range of stakeholders, including civil society, the private sector, and marginalized communities," Dr. Mwansa explained. "They also promote a balanced approach to development, addressing social, economic, and environmental dimensions in an integrated and holistic manner."

A student in the front row spoke up, her voice filled with determination. "How can Zambia ensure effective implementation and monitoring of its national development plans?"

Dr. Mwansa nodded, acknowledging the importance of robust implementation and monitoring mechanisms in translating plans into tangible results. "Ensuring effective implementation and monitoring of national development plans requires strong political commitment, institutional capacity, and stakeholder engagement," he replied, transitioning to a slide showing examples of best practices in implementation and monitoring.

"This includes establishing clear targets, timelines, and responsibilities for implementation, as well as mobilizing financial resources, technical expertise, and political support," Dr. Mwansa explained. "It also involves putting in place robust monitoring and evaluation systems to track progress, identify bottlenecks, and adjust strategies as needed."

He then displayed graphs showing the potential impact of effective implementation and monitoring on various indicators, from poverty reduction to economic growth, from social inclusion to environmental sustainability. "Moreover, effective implementation and monitoring are not just technical processes; they are also about building trust, fostering accountability, and empowering citizens to participate in the development process," Dr. Mwansa concluded. "By embracing innovation, collaboration, and inclusivity, Zambia can unlock the full potential of its national development plans to drive positive change and improve the lives of all Zambians."

As the lecture concluded, Dr. Mwansa left the students with a final thought. "National development plans are the compass and roadmap that guide Zambia's journey towards a brighter future. By embracing ambition, resilience, and collaboration, we can navigate the challenges and opportunities of development and build a more prosperous, equitable, and sustainable Zambia for all."

The students left the room, their minds buzzing with newfound insights into the intricacies of Zambia's national development planning process. They understood that by championing inclusive and participatory approaches, they could contribute to shaping a future where Zambia's development aspirations are realized through collective action and shared commitment.

Dr. Mwansa watched them go, filled with hope for the impact they would make as future leaders, policymakers, and changemakers in Zambia's journey towards a brighter tomorrow. He knew that with their passion, determination, and commitment to inclusive development, they would continue to drive progress and shape policies that improve the lives of all Zambians, today and in the years to come.

Policy Coherence for Development in Zambia

In the hushed ambiance of the lecture hall, Dr. Mwansa assumed his position at the lectern, prepared to explore the concept of policy coherence for development in Zambia. Anticipation lingered in the air as eager minds awaited enlightenment on the intricacies of aligning policies for sustainable progress.

"Good afternoon, everyone," Dr. Mwansa greeted, his voice resonating with authority and warmth. "Today, we embark on a journey through the realm of policy coherence for development, where synergy is forged, and pathways to progress are illuminated."

With a click, the screen flickered to life, displaying a montage of images illustrating Zambia's diverse policy landscape and its impact on development. "Policy coherence for development is about ensuring that policies across different sectors are aligned and mutually reinforcing, so they can collectively contribute to Zambia's development goals," Dr. Mwansa elucidated. "It involves integrating economic, social, environmental, and governance objectives into policymaking processes, thereby maximizing the positive impact of policies on sustainable development outcomes."

The next slide showcased examples of policy coherence in action, from strategies to promote inclusive growth and reduce inequalities to initiatives to enhance environmental sustainability and strengthen governance. "Policy coherence is essential for addressing the interconnected challenges facing Zambia, such as poverty, inequality, climate change, and governance deficits," Dr. Mwansa continued. "By fostering synergy and integration among policies, Zambia can enhance the effectiveness, efficiency, and sustainability of its development efforts."

A student raised her hand, her voice tinged with curiosity. "What are some of the key principles and approaches to achieving policy coherence for development?"

"An excellent question," Dr. Mwansa replied, bringing up a slide illustrating the key principles and approaches. "Key principles include coordination, integration, and alignment of policies, as well as participation, inclusivity, and accountability in policymaking processes."

He then displayed images of policymakers collaborating across sectors, stakeholders engaging in dialogue, and communities participating in decision-making, highlighting the importance of inclusive and participatory approaches to policy coherence. "Moreover, achieving policy coherence requires robust institutional mechanisms, effective coordination structures, and coherent planning processes," Dr. Mwansa explained. "It also involves promoting a culture of collaboration, innovation, and learning among policymakers, practitioners, and stakeholders."

A student in the front row spoke up, her voice filled with determination. "How can Zambia overcome the challenges and barriers to policy coherence for development?"

Dr. Mwansa nodded, acknowledging the complexities and obstacles inherent in achieving policy coherence. "Overcoming the challenges to policy coherence requires political will, institutional capacity, and stakeholder engagement," he replied, transitioning to a slide showing examples of strategies to promote policy coherence.

"This includes establishing clear mandates, roles, and responsibilities for coordinating bodies, as well as enhancing data collection, analysis, and dissemination to inform policy-making," Dr. Mwansa explained. "It also involves promoting dialogue, consultation, and collaboration among government agencies, civil society organizations, and the private sector, as well as fostering partnerships with international development partners and regional organizations."

He then displayed graphs showing the potential impact of policy coherence on various indicators, from economic growth to social inclusion, from environmental sustainability to governance effectiveness. "Moreover, policy coherence is not just about achieving short-term objectives; it is also about building resilience, promoting sustainability, and fostering inclusive development," Dr. Mwansa concluded. "By embracing innovation, collaboration, and inclusivity, Zambia can unlock the full potential of policy coherence to drive positive change and improve the lives of all Zambians."

As the lecture concluded, Dr. Mwansa left the students with a final thought. "Policy coherence for development is the compass that guides Zambia's journey towards a brighter future. By embracing ambition, resilience, and collaboration, we can navigate the complexities and challenges of development and build a more prosperous, equitable, and sustainable Zambia for all."

The students left the room, their minds buzzing with newfound insights into the importance of policy coherence for development. They understood that by championing inclusive and participatory approaches, they could contribute to shaping a future where policies work in harmony to achieve Zambia's development aspirations.

Dr. Mwansa watched them go, filled with hope for the impact they would make as future leaders, policymakers, and changemakers in Zambia's journey towards a brighter tomorrow. He knew that with their passion, determination, and commitment to inclusive development, they would continue to drive progress and shape policies that improve the lives of all Zambians, today and in the years to come.

15

Chapter 15: Case Studies in Development

Successful Development Interventions in Zambia

In the twilight hours of the lecture hall, Dr. Mwansa stood before his students, prepared to unravel the tales of successful development interventions in Zambia. The air was charged with anticipation as eager minds awaited the unveiling of stories showcasing progress, innovation, and resilience.

"Good afternoon, everyone," Dr. Mwansa began, his voice resonating with enthusiasm and anticipation. "Today, we embark on a journey through the realm of successful development interventions in Zambia, where ingenuity, perseverance, and collaboration have transformed challenges into opportunities."

With a click, the screen illuminated with a montage of images capturing moments of triumph and transformation across Zambia's diverse landscapes. "Successful development interventions are the culmination of visionary leadership, community engagement, and strategic partnerships," Dr. Mwansa elucidated. "They exemplify the power of innovation, resilience, and inclusivity in driving positive change and improving the lives of all Zambians."

The next slide showcased examples of successful interventions, from initiatives to promote education and healthcare to projects aimed at enhancing agricultural productivity and environmental sustainability. "Each success story represents a beacon of hope and inspiration, demonstrating the transformative impact of targeted interventions on individuals, communities, and the nation as a whole," Dr. Mwansa continued. "From rural villages to urban centers, from grassroots initiatives to large-scale programs, these interventions have left an indelible mark on Zambia's development trajectory."

A student raised her hand, her voice tinged with curiosity. "What are some of the key ingredients for success in development interventions?"

"An excellent question," Dr. Mwansa replied, bringing up a slide illustrating the key ingredients for success. "Key ingredients include strong leadership, community ownership, and stakeholder engagement, as well as innovation, adaptability, and sustainability."

He then displayed images of local leaders championing development initiatives, communities collaborating on project implementation, and stakeholders working together to overcome challenges, highlighting the importance of partnership and participation in achieving success. "Moreover, successful interventions are characterized by a clear vision, realistic goals, and effective monitoring and evaluation mechanisms," Dr. Mwansa explained. "They also prioritize inclusivity, equity, and social justice, ensuring that the benefits of development are shared by all."

A student in the front row spoke up, her voice filled with determination. "How can Zambia replicate and scale up successful interventions to achieve broader impact?"

Dr. Mwansa nodded, acknowledging the importance of replication and scaling in maximizing the impact of successful interventions. "Replicating and scaling successful interventions require strategic planning, resource mobilization, and institutional support," he replied, transitioning to a slide showing examples of strategies for replication and scaling.

"This includes documenting best practices, sharing lessons learned, and building capacity among stakeholders to replicate successful models," Dr. Mwansa explained. "It also involves mobilizing financial resources, technical expertise, and political support to scale up successful interventions and ensure their sustainability."

He then displayed graphs showing the potential impact of replication and scaling on various indicators, from poverty reduction to social inclusion, from environmental conservation to economic growth. "Moreover, replication and scaling are not just about achieving numerical targets; they are also about fostering innovation, promoting learning, and catalyzing systemic change," Dr. Mwansa concluded. "By embracing collaboration, innovation, and inclusivity, Zambia can replicate and scale successful interventions to drive positive change and build a more resilient, prosperous, and sustainable future for all."

As the lecture concluded, Dr. Mwansa left the students with a final thought. "Successful development interventions are the building blocks of Zambia's development journey.

By embracing innovation, collaboration, and inclusivity, we can replicate and scale these interventions to unlock the full potential of Zambia's people and resources, and build a brighter future for all."

The students left the room, their minds ablaze with inspiration and determination. They understood that by championing innovative solutions, fostering collaboration, and promoting inclusivity, they could contribute to replicating and scaling successful interventions to drive positive change and improve the lives of all Zambians.

Dr. Mwansa watched them go, filled with hope for the impact they would make as future leaders, policymakers, and changemakers in Zambia's journey towards a brighter tomorrow. He knew that with their passion, determination, and commitment to inclusive development, they would continue to drive progress and shape policies that improve the lives of all Zambians, today and in the years to come.

Lessons from Failed Projects in Zambia

In the dimly lit lecture hall, Dr. Mwansa took center stage, ready to unravel the lessons learned from failed projects in Zambia. Anticipation crackled in the air as students leaned forward, eager to glean insights from setbacks and failures that could illuminate the path forward.

"Good afternoon, everyone," Dr. Mwansa began, his voice carrying a tone of introspection and resilience. "Today, we delve into the realm of failed projects in Zambia, where challenges, setbacks, and disappointments have provided invaluable lessons for future endeavors."

With a click, the screen flickered to life, displaying a montage of images capturing moments of struggle and adversity across Zambia's diverse landscapes. "Failed projects are not just setbacks; they are opportunities for reflection, learning, and growth," Dr. Mwansa elucidated. "They offer insights into the complexities and challenges of development, as well as the importance of adaptive management, resilience, and innovation."

The next slide showcased examples of failed projects, from infrastructure initiatives plagued by cost overruns to social programs hampered by mismanagement and corruption. "Each failure represents a missed opportunity and a painful reminder of the need for vigilance, accountability, and transparency in development efforts," Dr. Mwansa continued. "From technical miscalculations to governance failures, these projects have left lasting scars on Zambia's development landscape, underscoring the importance of careful planning, stakeholder engagement, and risk management."

A student raised her hand, her voice tinged with curiosity. "What are some of the key reasons for the failure of projects in Zambia?"

"An excellent question," Dr. Mwansa replied, bringing up a slide illustrating the key reasons for failure. "Key reasons include inadequate planning, insufficient stakeholder engagement, poor governance, and corruption, as well as external factors such as economic shocks, natural disasters, and political instability."

He then displayed images of project sites marred by delays and setbacks, communities disillusioned by broken promises, and stakeholders grappling with the aftermath of failure, highlighting the human cost of development setbacks. "Moreover, failed projects often result from a lack of accountability, transparency, and oversight, as well as a failure to adapt to changing circumstances and emerging challenges," Dr. Mwansa explained. "They also underscore the importance of addressing root causes such as poverty, inequality, and governance deficits, which can undermine the effectiveness and sustainability of development interventions."

A student in the front row spoke up, her voice filled with determination. "How can Zambia learn from failed projects and prevent similar mistakes in the future?"

Dr. Mwansa nodded, acknowledging the importance of learning from failure to inform future action. "Learning from failed projects requires humility, introspection, and a willingness to confront uncomfortable truths," he replied, transitioning to a slide showing examples of strategies for learning from failure.

"This includes conducting rigorous post-mortem evaluations to identify root causes, lessons learned, and opportunities for improvement," Dr. Mwansa explained. "It also involves fostering a culture of transparency, accountability, and continuous learning among policymakers, practitioners, and stakeholders, as well as promoting dialogue, collaboration, and knowledge sharing across sectors and disciplines."

He then displayed graphs showing the potential impact of learning from failure on various indicators, from project success rates to institutional effectiveness, from public trust to development outcomes. "Moreover, learning from failure is not just about avoiding mistakes; it is also about building resilience, fostering innovation, and strengthening governance," Dr. Mwansa concluded. "By embracing humility, adaptability, and collaboration, Zambia can transform setbacks into opportunities, and build a more resilient, inclusive, and sustainable

future for all."

As the lecture concluded, Dr. Mwansa left the students with a final thought. "Failed projects are not the end of the road; they are the beginning of a journey towards greater understanding, resilience, and progress. By embracing the lessons learned from failure, we can navigate the complexities and challenges of development with wisdom, compassion, and determination."

The students left the room, their minds ablaze with new-found insights into the importance of learning from failure. They understood that by championing transparency, account-ability, and adaptability, they could contribute to shaping a future where setbacks are transformed into opportunities for growth and innovation.

Dr. Mwansa watched them go, filled with hope for the impact they would make as future leaders, policymakers, and changemakers in Zambia's journey towards a brighter tomor-row. He knew that with their passion, determination, and commitment to inclusive development, they would continue to drive progress and shape policies that improve the lives of all Zambians, today and in the years to come.

Comparative Development Approaches: Zambia vs. Other Nations

In the lecture hall bathed in a soft glow, Dr. Mwansa stood poised at the lectern, prepared to unravel the intricate tapestry of comparative development approaches between Zambia and other nations. Anticipation rippled through the room as students leaned in, eager to grasp the nuances of Zambia's developmental journey in the global context.

"Good afternoon, everyone," Dr. Mwansa began, his voice carrying a tone of curiosity and exploration. "Today, we embark on a comparative exploration of development approaches, where Zambia's trajectory intertwines with the experiences of nations around the world."

With a click, the screen flickered to life, displaying a mosaic of images depicting the diverse landscapes and cultures of nations across the globe. "Comparative development approaches offer valuable insights into the contextual factors, policy choices, and strategies that shape development outcomes," Dr. Mwansa elucidated. "By examining Zambia's experiences alongside those of other nations, we can glean lessons, identify opportunities, and inform future action."

The next slide showcased examples of comparative development approaches, from strategies to promote economic growth and poverty reduction to initiatives aimed at enhancing social inclusion and environmental sustainability. "Each nation's developmental journey is unique, shaped by historical legacies, geographic realities, and socio-political dynamics," Dr. Mwansa continued. "Yet, common threads of innovation, resilience, and collaboration bind our shared aspirations for a better future."

A student raised her hand, her voice tinged with curiosity. "What are some key similarities and differences between Zambia and other nations in terms of development approaches?"

"An excellent question," Dr. Mwansa replied, bringing up a slide illustrating key similarities and differences. "Key similarities include shared challenges such as poverty, inequality, and environmental degradation, as well as common goals such as economic prosperity, social justice, and environmental sustainability."

He then displayed images highlighting Zambia's efforts to address these challenges alongside examples from other nations facing similar struggles, underscoring the interconnectedness of global development issues. "Moreover, key differences stem from contextual factors such as resource endowments, governance structures, and cultural norms," Dr. Mwansa explained. "These differences shape the priorities, strategies, and outcomes of development efforts, yet they also offer opportunities for mutual learning, collaboration, and innovation."

A student in the front row spoke up, her voice filled with determination. "How can Zambia leverage comparative development approaches to inform its own strategies and policies?"

Dr. Mwansa nodded, acknowledging the potential of comparative analysis to inform Zambia's development trajectory. "Leveraging comparative development approaches requires openness, humility, and a willingness to learn from diverse experiences," he replied, transitioning to a slide showing examples of strategies for leveraging comparative analysis.

"This includes conducting rigorous comparative studies, engaging in dialogue and knowledge exchange with counterparts in other nations, and adapting successful approaches to suit Zambia's unique context," Dr. Mwansa explained. "It also involves fostering partnerships, collaborations, and networks across borders, sectors, and disciplines, as well as promoting a culture of innovation, experimentation, and continuous learning."

He then displayed graphs showing the potential impact of leveraging comparative analysis on various indicators, from policy effectiveness to development outcomes, from institutional capacity to global competitiveness. "Moreover, leveraging comparative development approaches is not just about borrowing best practices; it is also about contributing to global knowledge, sharing Zambia's experiences, and shaping collective solutions to shared challenges," Dr. Mwansa concluded. "By embracing diversity, collaboration, and innovation, Zambia can draw inspiration from the experiences of other nations and chart a course towards a more prosperous, equitable, and sustainable future for all."

As the lecture concluded, Dr. Mwansa left the students with a final thought. "Comparative development approaches offer a kaleidoscope of perspectives, insights, and possibilities. By embracing humility, curiosity, and collaboration, we can unlock the transformative power of comparative analysis to drive positive change and shape a brighter future for Zambia and the world."

The students left the room, their minds ablaze with new-found insights into the importance of comparative analysis in shaping development strategies. They understood that by embracing diversity, collaboration, and innovation, they could contribute to building bridges of understanding and cooperation that transcend borders and cultures.

Dr. Mwansa watched them go, filled with hope for the impact they would make as future leaders, policymakers, and changemakers in Zambia's journey towards a brighter tomorrow. He knew that with their passion, determination, and commitment to inclusive development, they would continue to drive progress and shape policies that improve the lives of all Zambians, today and in the years to come.

Regional Development Case Studies within Zambia

In the hushed confines of the lecture hall, Dr. Mwansa stood poised at the lectern, ready to delve into the regional development case studies within Zambia. The anticipation in the room was palpable as students eagerly awaited insights into the diverse regional dynamics shaping Zambia's developmental landscape.

"Good afternoon, everyone," Dr. Mwansa began, his voice resonating with a sense of exploration and discovery. "Today, we embark on a journey through the regional development case studies within Zambia, where local contexts, challenges, and opportunities intersect to shape unique developmental pathways."

With a click, the screen illuminated, casting a spotlight on a map of Zambia adorned with markers representing regions rich in history, culture, and economic activities. "Regional development case studies offer invaluable insights into the complexities and nuances of Zambia's developmental journey," Dr. Mwansa elucidated. "By examining the successes, challenges, and lessons learned from different regions, we can glean actionable knowledge to inform targeted interventions and policies."

The next slide showcased examples of regional development case studies, from initiatives promoting agricultural productivity in rural areas to projects fostering entrepreneurship and innovation in urban centers. "Each region of Zambia possesses its own distinct characteristics, resources, and development priorities," Dr. Mwansa continued. "Yet, common threads of resilience, ingenuity, and community spirit bind these diverse landscapes in their quest for progress and prosperity."

A student raised her hand, her voice tinged with curiosity. "What are some key factors influencing regional development disparities within Zambia?"

"An excellent question," Dr. Mwansa replied, bringing up a slide illustrating key factors. "Key factors include geographic location, natural resource endowments, infrastructure development, governance structures, and historical legacies."

He then displayed images depicting the varied landscapes and economic activities across Zambia's regions, underscoring the interconnectedness of factors shaping regional development disparities. "Moreover, regional development disparities stem from unequal access to resources, opportunities, and services, as well as differential levels of investment, infrastructure, and connectivity," Dr. Mwansa explained. "These disparities pose challenges to inclusive and sustainable development, yet they also offer opportunities for targeted interventions, strategic investments, and collaborative initiatives."

A student in the front row spoke up, her voice filled with determination. "How can Zambia address regional development disparities and promote inclusive growth across all regions?"

Dr. Mwansa nodded, acknowledging the importance of addressing regional disparities to foster equitable development. "Addressing regional development disparities requires a multifaceted approach that combines targeted interventions, strategic investments, and inclusive policies," he replied, transitioning to a slide showing examples of strategies for promoting inclusive growth.

"This includes promoting regional integration and connectivity, investing in infrastructure and basic services, and supporting local entrepreneurship and innovation," Dr. Mwansa explained. "It also involves fostering partnerships, collaborations, and networks among stakeholders in government, civil society, and the private sector, as well as empowering communities to participate in decision-making and development processes."

He then displayed graphs showing the potential impact of addressing regional disparities on various indicators, from poverty reduction to economic growth, from social inclusion to environmental sustainability. "Moreover, addressing regional development disparities is not just about achieving numerical targets; it is also about fostering social cohesion, building resilience, and strengthening governance," Dr. Mwansa concluded. "By embracing diversity, collaboration, and innovation, Zambia can harness the collective potential of all its regions to build a more prosperous, equitable, and sustainable future for all."

As the lecture concluded, Dr. Mwansa left the students with a final thought. "Regional development case studies offer windows into the soul of Zambia, revealing the aspirations, challenges, and triumphs of its diverse people and landscapes. By embracing humility, empathy, and collaboration, we can transform regional disparities into opportunities for growth, innovation, and shared prosperity."

The students left the room, their minds abuzz with newfound insights into the regional dynamics shaping Zambia's developmental landscape. They understood that by championing inclusivity, collaboration, and innovation, they could contribute to building bridges of understanding and cooperation that spanned across Zambia's diverse regions.

Dr. Mwansa watched them go, filled with hope for the impact they would make as future leaders, policymakers, and changemakers in Zambia's journey towards a brighter tomorrow. He knew that with their passion, determination, and commitment to inclusive development, they would continue to drive progress and shape policies that improve the lives of all Zambians, today and in the years to come.

Grassroots and Community-Led Initiatives in Zambia

In the cozy ambiance of the lecture hall, Dr. Mwansa took center stage, ready to delve into the grassroots and community-led initiatives shaping Zambia's developmental landscape. Anticipation filled the room as students leaned forward, eager to explore the grassroots movements driving change from the ground up.

"Good afternoon, everyone," Dr. Mwansa began, his voice infused with enthusiasm and admiration for the grassroots efforts transforming Zambia. "Today, we shine a spotlight on the grassroots and community-led initiatives that are igniting change and fostering empowerment across Zambia."

With a click, the screen illuminated, showcasing a montage of images depicting community gatherings, volunteer projects, and local innovations flourishing in Zambia's diverse landscapes. "Grassroots and community-led initiatives embody the spirit of resilience, innovation, and collective action," Dr. Mwansa elucidated. "They harness the power of local knowledge, resources, and networks to address pressing challenges and seize opportunities for development."

The next slide displayed examples of grassroots and community-led initiatives, from women's cooperatives promoting entrepreneurship to youth-led movements advocating for social justice and environmental conservation. "Each initiative represents a beacon of hope and a testament to the transformative potential of bottom-up approaches to development," Dr. Mwansa continued. "They empower communities to take ownership of their futures, build resilience, and drive sustainable change from within."

A student raised her hand, her voice brimming with curiosity. "What are some key characteristics of successful grassroots and community-led initiatives in Zambia?"

"An excellent question," Dr. Mwansa replied, bringing up a slide illustrating key characteristics. "Successful grassroots and community-led initiatives exhibit characteristics such as local ownership, inclusivity, participatory decision-making, adaptability, and sustainability."

He then displayed images showcasing the diverse faces and voices driving grassroots initiatives across Zambia, underscoring the importance of community engagement and collaboration. "Moreover, successful initiatives leverage local knowledge, resources, and networks to tailor interventions to the unique needs and aspirations of communities," Dr. Mwansa explained. "They also foster partnerships, collaborations, and networks among stakeholders in government, civil society, and the private sector to amplify impact and scale up successful models."

A student in the front row spoke up, her voice filled with determination. "How can Zambia support and strengthen grassroots and community-led initiatives to drive sustainable development?"

Dr. Mwansa nodded, acknowledging the critical role of support in nurturing grassroots initiatives. "Supporting and strengthening grassroots and community-led initiatives requires a holistic approach that combines policy reforms, capacity building, and resource mobilization," he replied, transitioning to a slide showing examples of strategies for support.

"This includes creating an enabling environment for civil society organizations, community-based groups, and social enterprises to thrive," Dr. Mwansa explained. "It also involves providing technical assistance, training, and mentorship to build the capacity of local leaders and organizations, as well as mobilizing financial resources and leveraging partnerships to sustain and scale up successful initiatives."

He then displayed graphs showing the potential impact of supporting grassroots initiatives on various indicators, from community resilience to social cohesion, from economic empowerment to environmental sustainability. "Moreover, supporting grassroots and community-led initiatives is not just about achieving short-term outcomes; it is also about fostering long-term resilience, innovation, and self-reliance," Dr. Mwansa concluded. "By embracing diversity, collaboration, and empowerment, Zambia can unleash the transformative potential of its grassroots movements to build a more inclusive, equitable, and sustainable future for all."

As the lecture concluded, Dr. Mwansa left the students with a final thought. "Grassroots and community-led initiatives are the heartbeat of Zambia's development, pulsating with the energy and creativity of its people. By embracing humility, empathy, and collaboration, we can amplify the voices of communities, unlock their potential, and co-create a future where every Zambian thrives."

The students left the room, their minds ablaze with new-found insights into the power of grassroots initiatives to drive change. They understood that by championing inclusivity, empowerment, and collaboration, they could contribute to building a more resilient, equitable, and sustainable Zambia for generations to come.

Dr. Mwansa watched them go, filled with hope for the impact they would make as future leaders, policymakers, and changemakers in Zambia's journey towards a brighter tomorrow. He knew that with their passion, determination, and commitment to grassroots empowerment, they would continue to drive progress and shape policies that improve the lives of all Zambians, today and in the years to come.

Future Directions in Zambian Developmental Studies

In the tranquil setting of the lecture hall, Dr. Mwansa stood before his attentive audience, ready to explore the future directions of Zambian developmental studies. Excitement tinged the air as students eagerly awaited insights into the evolving landscape of development in Zambia.

"Good afternoon, everyone," Dr. Mwansa began, his voice filled with anticipation for the journey ahead. "Today, we embark on a voyage into the future of Zambian developmental studies, where innovation, collaboration, and resilience converge to shape a brighter tomorrow."

With a click, the screen illuminated, revealing a vision of possibilities for the future of development in Zambia. "The future of Zambian developmental studies holds boundless opportunities for innovation, adaptation, and transformation," Dr. Mwansa elucidated. "It is a future where interdisciplinary approaches, technology, and participatory methodologies converge to address complex challenges and unlock new pathways to progress."

The next slide showcased examples of future directions in Zambian developmental studies, from harnessing emerging technologies to promote sustainable agriculture to fostering inclusive governance frameworks that amplify citizen voices and empower marginalized communities. "The future of Zambian developmental studies is characterized by a shift towards holistic, contextually relevant approaches that prioritize equity, sustainability, and resilience," Dr. Mwansa continued. "It is a future where partnerships, collaborations, and networks across sectors and disciplines drive collective action and shared impact."

A student raised her hand, her voice tinged with curiosity. "What are some key trends shaping the future of Zambian developmental studies?"

"An excellent question," Dr. Mwansa replied, bringing up a slide illustrating key trends. "Key trends shaping the future of Zambian developmental studies include the integration of digital technologies, data-driven decision-making, participatory methodologies, and a focus on inclusive and sustainable development."

He then displayed images showcasing examples of innovative projects and initiatives that exemplify these emerging trends, underscoring their potential to drive positive change and catalyze progress. "Moreover, the future of Zambian developmental studies is characterized by a growing recognition of the importance of indigenous knowledge, cultural heritage, and community-led approaches in shaping development pathways," Dr. Mwansa explained. "It is a future where diversity, inclusion, and empowerment are not just buzzwords but guiding principles that inform policies, practices, and priorities."

A student in the front row spoke up, her voice filled with determination. "How can we as future leaders and changemakers contribute to shaping the future of Zambian developmental studies?"

Dr. Mwansa nodded, acknowledging the pivotal role of the next generation in driving change. "Contributing to shaping the future of Zambian developmental studies requires vision, courage, and a commitment to lifelong learning," he replied, transitioning to a slide showing examples of strategies for contribution.

"This includes embracing interdisciplinary approaches, cultivating empathy and cultural competence, and leveraging emerging technologies and methodologies to address complex challenges," Dr. Mwansa explained. "It also involves fostering partnerships, collaborations, and networks with diverse stakeholders, from government and civil society to academia and the private sector, as well as empowering communities to co-create solutions that reflect their needs, aspirations, and values."

He then displayed graphs showing the potential impact of collective action on shaping the future of Zambian developmental studies, from innovation and resilience to equity and sustainability. "Moreover, shaping the future of Zambian developmental studies is not just about achieving short-term outcomes; it is also about fostering a culture of continuous learning, adaptation, and resilience," Dr. Mwansa concluded. "By embracing curiosity, creativity, and collaboration, we can unlock the transformative potential of Zambian developmental studies to build a more inclusive, equitable, and sustainable

future for all."

As the lecture concluded, Dr. Mwansa left the students with a final thought. "The future of Zambian developmental studies is ours to shape, ours to mold, and ours to transform. By embracing humility, empathy, and collaboration, we can unleash the collective potential of our diverse talents, perspectives, and experiences to build a future where every Zambian thrives."

The students left the room, their minds ablaze with new-found insights into the possibilities that lie ahead. They understood that by embracing innovation, collaboration, and resilience, they could contribute to shaping a future where Zambian developmental studies serve as a beacon of hope and a catalyst for positive change.

Dr. Mwansa watched them go, filled with hope for the impact they would make as future leaders, policymakers, and changemakers in Zambia's journey towards a brighter tomorrow. He knew that with their passion, determination, and commitment to inclusive and sustainable development, they would continue to drive progress and shape policies that improve the lives of all Zambians, today and in the years to come.

About the Author

Goodson Mumba is a multifaceted individual known for his diverse expertise and prolific contributions across various fields. As an infopreneur, thought leader, and spiritual leader, he has inspired countless individuals through his insightful teachings and impactful writings. Mumba is also an accomplished author, with several notable works to his name, including "Understanding Corporate Worship," "The Years I Spent in a Week," "Management By Harmony," "The CEO's Diary," "Change to Change" and "Creative Thinking for results" His literary works span topics ranging from business management to personal development and spirituality, reflecting his broad range of interests and insights.

With a Master of Business Leadership (MBL) and a Bachelor of Arts in Theology (BTh), Mumba brings a unique blend of business acumen and spiritual wisdom to his work. His educational background is further enriched by a Group Diploma in Management Studies, providing him with a solid foundation in organizational dynamics and leadership principles. Additionally, Mumba holds diplomas in Education

Psychology, Leadership and Management Styles, Organizational Behaviour, Financial Accounting, Economic Growth and Development, and Project Management, showcasing his commitment to continuous learning and professional development.

Mumba's expertise extends beyond traditional academic disciplines, encompassing areas such as Neuro-Linguistic Programming (NLP) and Positive Psychology. His diverse skill set is complemented by a range of certifications, including Creative Problem Solving and Decision Making, Life Coaching Fundamentals and Techniques, Professional Life Coaching, and Performance Management System Design. These certifications reflect Mumba's dedication to equipping himself with the tools and knowledge necessary to empower others and drive positive change.

As an author, Mumba's writings reflect his deep understanding of human nature, organizational dynamics, and spiritual principles. His works offer practical insights, actionable strategies, and inspirational guidance for individuals seeking personal growth, professional success, and spiritual fulfillment. Mumba's holistic approach to life and leadership resonates with readers worldwide, making him a respected figure in both the business and spiritual communities.

Overall, Goodson Mumba's diverse background, extensive knowledge, and profound insights make him a sought-after speaker, mentor, and author. His commitment to excellence, lifelong learning, and service to others continues to inspire individuals to unlock their full potential and lead lives of purpose and significance.

Goodson Mumba is renowned for initiating the concept of Management by Harmony, revolutionizing traditional management practices with a focus on balanced and holistic approaches. He has authored two influential books on this subject: "Introduction to Management by Harmony" and its sequel, "Management by Harmony."

Mumba's work has significantly impacted the field, offering innovative strategies for fostering organizational harmony and efficiency. His contributions continue to shape contemporary management theories and practices.